Cambridge Elements

Elements on Women in the History of Philosophy
edited by
Jacqueline Broad
Monash University

HARRIET TAYLOR MILL

Helen McCabe
University of Nottingham

CAMBRIDGE
UNIVERSITY PRESS

CAMBRIDGE
UNIVERSITY PRESS

Shaftesbury Road, Cambridge CB2 8EA, United Kingdom

One Liberty Plaza, 20th Floor, New York, NY 10006, USA

477 Williamstown Road, Port Melbourne, VIC 3207, Australia

314–321, 3rd Floor, Plot 3, Splendor Forum, Jasola District Centre, New Delhi – 110025, India

103 Penang Road, #05–06/07, Visioncrest Commercial, Singapore 238467

Cambridge University Press is part of Cambridge University Press & Assessment, a department of the University of Cambridge.

We share the University's mission to contribute to society through the pursuit of education, learning and research at the highest international levels of excellence.

www.cambridge.org
Information on this title: www.cambridge.org/9781009156837

DOI: 10.1017/9781009156844

First published 2023

A catalogue record for this publication is available from the British Library.

ISBN 978-1-009-15683-7 Paperback
ISSN 2634-4645 (online)
ISSN 2634-4637 (print)

Harriet Taylor Mill

Elements on Women in the History of Philosophy

DOI: 10.1017/9781009156844
First published online: February 2023

Helen McCabe
University of Nottingham

Author for correspondence: Helen McCabe, helen.mccabe@nottingham.ac.uk

Abstract: Harriet Taylor Mill is an overlooked figure in the history of political philosophy, ethics, economics and politics, overshadowed by the fame of her writing partner, and eventual husband, John Stuart Mill. Given that they met at a very early age (when Taylor Mill was twenty-two), and wrote together for over a quarter of a century, it can be hard to distinguish what is 'hers' and what is 'his'. Indeed, maybe we should consider much of Mill's canon as being 'theirs'. Taylor Mill inputted into some extremely famous works, including *On Liberty*, and her thought, impact and legacy are well worth charting. This Element explores her contribution to political theory, ethics, political economy and political reform. It draws on close textual analysis of 'her' works and those of Mill (including manuscripts unpublished in her lifetime, and correspondence), as well as interrogating his description of their co-authoring relationship.

Keywords: feminism, Harriet Taylor Mill, John Stuart Mill, liberalism, utilitarianism

ISBNs: 9781009156837 (PB), 9781009156844 (OC)
ISSNs: 2634-4645 (online), 2634-4637 (print)

Contents

1 Introduction

Harriet Taylor Mill is a somewhat forgotten figure in the history of political thought, even though *The Enfranchisement of Women* (1851) alone should earn her a place in the history of feminism, as should her short (unpublished) essay *On Marriage* (1833), and the pieces she co-authored with John Stuart Mill (1846–51) on domestic violence (by intimate partners, parents and employers) and other abuses of power. Her legacy has, however, been overshadowed by her co-authoring, and romantic, relationship with Mill, which produced much more than a series of newspaper articles. Indeed, Mill says he and Taylor Mill wrote the whole of *On Liberty* together. Given the fame, and importance, of this foundational liberal text, Taylor Mill ought to be better recognised in the canon of political theory more broadly. She was an unwavering champion of personal liberty and the need to freely develop our individuality so long as we do not cause unhappiness to others. She was an ardent egalitarian and democrat, in terms of personal relationships, civil rights, and political economy. She had a rich and nuanced understanding of happiness, and wrote insightful and interesting pieces on ethics, political philosophy, religion and economics. Although some of her arguments and insights have been surpassed by more recent writers, her central concerns remain of contemporary relevance.

The main sections of this Element will consider different elements of Taylor Mill's philosophical work and contribution. For the remainder of this introduction, I will give a biographical account of her life and work, as she is unlikely to be well-known to most readers.

Harriet Taylor Mill was actually never known by that name. She was born Harriet Hardy, became Harriet Taylor and after being widowed became Harriet Mill. (Indeed, according to the conventions of the time, she was Miss Hardy then Mrs John Taylor and then Mrs John Stuart Mill.) But calling her Taylor Mill helps distinguish her from both her husbands, and from her daughter, Helen Taylor (herself a feminist campaigner and activist).

Taylor Mill was born, in London, on 8 October 1807. Her father, originally from Yorkshire, was a gynaecologist (or 'man-midwife', as her birth certificate records).[1] She had four brothers and a sister and, like most women of her class in that period, was educated at home. She learned several languages, read widely in history, literature and philosophy, and kept abreast of current events. On 14 March 1826, at the age of eighteen, she married John Taylor, a wholesale 'druggist or "drysalter"' eleven years her senior.[2] He too had radical and 'free-

---

[1] Mill-Taylor Archive, *London School of Economics Library Archive and Special Collections*, Box III.

[2] See Hayek, *John Stuart Mill and Harriet Taylor*, 24.

thinking' sympathies, becoming a founder member of the Reform Club in 1836 (which was intended as the headquarters of the Liberal Party, and a home for Radicals and Whigs who had supported the Great Reform Act of 1832) and being involved in the affairs of the new University of London.[3]

The newly-weds mixed in radical circles, particularly the free-thinking congregation of Unitarian minister William Johnson Fox. They had three children in relatively short succession: Herbert (1827), Algernon (1830) and Helen (1831). Extant letters show Taylor Mill, at least, was very much in love, and happy in her married life. She wrote poetry and literary reviews, including of books on contemporary politics. Although her earliest remaining writings on women's rights post-date this, it seems likely she was already interested in questions around women's education; women's vulnerability to abuse and domination both by parents and by their husbands; and women's political, social and economic rights.[4] It was this last subject which brought Mill into her orbit, probably in the summer of 1830.[5]

Already a well-known radical writer, who went against his father James Mill on the question of female suffrage, Mill was then exploring a variety of views outside the radical-utilitarianism which he had been born and bred to champion.[6] This was, in part, the result of what he later called 'a crisis in my mental history',[7] caused by Mill's realisation that achieving all the reforms for which he was fighting would not make him, personally, happy. Worse, he felt his education had left him lacking any meaningful emotional capacity at all. His faith in his father and Jeremy Bentham's educational, political and ethical project faltered, and he was left in despair. Reading Samuel Taylor Coleridge's poetry, among other things, helped him recover, and he deliberately set about exploring different political views, from the conservatism of Coleridge and Thomas Carlyle through the socialism of the Saint-Simonians to the Unitarian radicalism of the circle surrounding Fox.

Taylor Mill had, at this time, been married for six years. Although Mill later insisted that it was a long time before their friendship became in any way 'intimate', they were undoubtedly drawn to each other from their first meeting.[8] They were soon exchanging frank opinions on marriage – and Mill was addressing his side of this correspondence to 'she to whom my life is devoted'.[9] Mill later recalled that, though people might assume Taylor Mill's feminism was what made him a champion of women's rights, it was rather that his own feminist opinions were the root of his attractiveness to her.[10]

---

[3] *Ibid.* [4] *Ibid.*, 26. [5] *Ibid.*, 23, 36–7. [6] Mill, *Autobiography*, 107, 137–91.
[7] *Ibid.*, 137–8. [8] *Ibid.*, 193. [9] Mill, *On Marriage*, 37. [10] Mill, *Autobiography*, 253.

By the autumn of 1833, things had come to a head. Taylor agreed to a trial separation, and Taylor Mill took her children to Paris, where Mill joined her (after some soul-searching on both sides, given how much this move would involve them both sacrificing).[11] They were extremely happy[12] – but divorce was impossible at this date, and both knew they were causing a great deal of unhappiness to Taylor.

Eventually, they determined on a utilitarian compromise – that which would secure most happiness for most people, including Taylor Mill's husband and children. She returned to London to live with Taylor, but, as she expressed it, was 'to neither of the two men more than a *Seelenfreundin*' (a 'soulmate').[13] She refused to give up 'the liberty of sight',[14] continuing to see Mill frequently, including travelling abroad with him. The original agreement was altered after a relatively short period, with Taylor Mill moving into her own home in Keston Heath in June 1834.[15] This seems to have been, in the main, a well-kept secret, with Taylor Mill's family (apart from her children) apparently unaware she no longer lived with her husband, directing, for example, all their letters to her marital address.[16] Generally, her relations with Taylor seem to have remained cordial, with the family meeting for birthdays and to celebrate Christmas, and her letters being addressed to 'my dear John'.[17] She also stayed with him when visiting London.[18]

This said, the course of her and Mill's love did not run entirely smoothly, and Taylor Mill evidently did not find the situation an easy one – in a letter probably from 1834 she wrote '[h]appiness has become to me a word without meaning', and in one probably from 1835 she refers to the 'petty annoyances' which were 'wearing and depressing not only to body but to mind' which she had 'on account of our relation', but Mill did not.[19] The compromise, though it endured, was evidently fragile, at least at the beginning: Taylor Mill yearned for a more complete relationship with Mill, but 'hesitate[d] about the rightfulness of, for my own pleasure, giving up my only earthly opportunity of "usefulness"' which was 'marked out as duty'. 'I should', she said, 'spoil four lives [i.e. her husband and three children] & injure others [i.e. her family]. Now I give pleasure around me, I make no one unhappy; & am happy tho' not happiest myself'.[20]

---

[11] See Mill, Letter 84, to Thomas Carlyle, 5 September 1833, *CW* XII, 174–5 and Mill, Letter 89, to William Johnson Fox, 5 and 6 November 1833, 185–90.

[12] Mill, Letter 89, 185–90. [13] See Hayek, *John Stuart Mill and Harriet Taylor*, 56.

[14] Mill, Letter 89, 186. [15] See Jacobs, 'Chronology', xlii.

[16] Though there was some gossip about Mill and Taylor Mill's relationship, see Hayek, *John Stuart Mill and Harriet Taylor*, 79–90.

[17] See, for example, Taylor Mill, *Complete Works*, 442.

[18] See Mill, *Autobiography*, 237, as well as indications in Taylor Mill's letters.

[19] Taylor Mill, *Complete Works*, 329–30. [20] *Ibid.*, 332.

Taylor Mill does not appear to have written anything in the remaining years of the 1830s, or for some time into the 1840s, with an eye to publication. Apart from some letters, her only remaining writing is a journal from the spring of 1839 when she travelled in Italy with her children and Mill.[21] (There are also some undated fragments in her manuscripts which might come from this period, and she may have contributed to Mill's unpublished letter about 'Enlightened Infidelity' from 1842.[22]) She was probably busy bringing up her children: her sons went to school, but her daughter Helen was educated at home. Her circumstances kept her out of most society, though this seems also to have been her inclination. She wrote to Mill: 'I know what the world is, and have not the least desire either to brave it or to court it', and to Taylor, of potential guests for Christmas, 'a very little society is most agreeable to me'.[23]

This said, Mill recalled that 'during many of the years of confidential friendship' they enjoyed in the 1830s and 1840s, 'all my published writings were as much her work as mine; her share constantly increasing as years advanced' because:

> When two persons have their thoughts and speculations completely in common; when all subjects of intellectual or moral interest are discussed between them in daily life, and probed to much greater depth than are usually or conveniently sounded in writings intended for general readers; when they set out from them same principles and arrive at their conclusions by processes pursued jointly, it is of little consequence in respect to the question of originality which of them holds the pen . . . the writings are the joint product of both.[24]

During the 1830s and 1840s, Mill was becoming increasingly well-known as an author. His first 'best-seller' was *System of Logic* (1843). His next 'hit', *Principles of Political Economy* (1848), was, he said, the first work in which Taylor Mill played 'a conspicuous part'.[25] She suggested the addition of a key chapter ('On the Probable Futurity of the Labouring Classes'), and the dichotomy it explores between the dependence and independence of working people. She also influenced the whole 'tone' of the book, and its efforts to make plain that the laws of production are pretty much 'fixed' by hard facts about the world (the finite nature of some resources, for instance), but the laws of distribution are human-made, and thus changeable and subject to considerations of justice.

---

[21] *Ibid.*, 170–5.   [22] *Ibid.*, 340.

[23] *Ibid.*, 333, 490. Of course, there could be something of sour grapes in this, given that Taylor Mill was cut off from society by her irregular relationship with her husband and with Mill. Her preference for little society, and a quiet life, however, seems to have also persisted after she married Mill.

[24] Mill, *Autobiography*, 251.   [25] *Ibid.*, 255.

Taylor vetoed Mill's plan to dedicate *Principles* to Taylor Mill, though the proposed inscription was included in some copies given to friends.[26]

Between 1846 and 1851 (spanning the time *Principles* was being written and first published (1847–8), and she and Mill were working on the second edition (1849)), Taylor Mill and Mill also worked together on a series of articles for the *Morning Chronicle* broadly engaging with themes around cruelty, violence and the tyrannical abuse of power. The first, about 'The Acquittal of Captain Johnstone', who had been charged 'with the brutal murders of three seamen under his command during a return voyage from China' deals with the poor judgment of juries and judges, as do several others.[27] 'The Suicide of Sarah Brown' highlights the issue of men being able to break the law (in this case regarding allowing a mother access to their illegitimate child, in others regarding domestic violence) with apparent impunity because of the bias of judges and juries.[28] These pieces show Taylor Mill's deep engagement with current events, and her anger at the injustice of the legal system and the apparent unconcern from most people (or at least most men) about cruelty and abuse of power (particularly towards those whom society rendered weaker, from employees through women and children to animals).

Taylor Mill suffered from bouts of illness throughout her life, as did Mill. Like many other middle- and upper-class people at the time, she often went to the coast, or to warmer regions of the continent, to try to improve her health. In 1849, she went to the French Pyrenean coastal resort of Pau, which was becoming increasingly popular with British people after the Scottish physician Alexander Taylor (no relation) recommended it as a cure for 'winter depression' and respiratory disease.

Even before she left for Pau, Taylor Mill was concerned about her husband's health, and offering advice over how to protect and improve it.[29] He continued to send poor reports of his physical condition throughout the spring.[30] Taylor Mill was torn between returning to London 'in the hopes of being to be of use' to him, and what she felt was her duty to stay in Pau to be with Mill, who had effectively lost his sight over the winter – doctors prescribed complete rest in a healthier climate as a cure.[31] She decided to stay on in Pau, spending around a month there looking after Mill.

On their return, Taylor Mill discovered that Taylor had been diagnosed with cancer. She moved back into the marital home to nurse him, fighting on his

---

[26] *Ibid.*, 257. [27] Taylor Mill and Mill, 'The Acquittal of Captain Johnstone', 865–6.
[28] Taylor Mill and Mill, 'The Suicide of Sarah Brown', 916–19.
[29] Taylor Mill, *Complete Works*, 489–90, 495. [30] *Ibid.*, 501.
[31] *Ibid.* Mill's sight loss was, fortunately, only temporary.

behalf for second opinions and new treatments, but ultimately she was unsuccessful. Taylor died on 18 July 1849.

It was during her period of mourning that Taylor Mill worked on *Enfranchisement of Women*. Mill sent her the notice of a meeting of American suffrage organisations (of which *Enfranchisement* is ostensibly a review) because he knew she was 'out of spirits' and hoped she might be cheered by it.[32] *Enfranchisement* praises not only most of the aims of the American suffrage organisations but also the way in which they are organised and led by women themselves. It contains radical arguments for both women's right to, and need to, vote. Although published anonymously, it seems to have been a relatively open secret that Taylor Mill penned it (with some involvement by Mill).[33]

Despite their criticisms of marriage as an institution, Mill and Taylor Mill married on 21 April 1851. Her two younger children were their witnesses, a sign that Taylor Mill's immediate family approved of her decision, even if Mill's family did not. (His brother George, in particular, was shocked that Taylor Mill would contemplate entering, again, into an institution she had so strongly criticised.[34]) Mill did his best to legally divest himself of the powers given to husbands in and by marriage while delighting in the fact of their union, addressing Taylor Mill in several letters as 'my darling wife'.[35] They moved to a house in Blackheath, Kent.

In the 1850s, both Taylor Mill and Mill suffered further ill health, including bouts of serious sickness from tuberculosis in the winter of 1853–4, which prompted them to make a list of topics they wanted to record their thoughts on before they died. These included '[d]ifferences of character (nation, race, age, sex, temperament). Love. Education of tastes. Religion de l'Avenir [religion of the future/religion of humanity]. Plato. Slander. Foundation of morals. Utility of religion. Socialism. Liberty. Doctrine that causation is will ... Family, & Conventional'.[36]

It is not clear how much work was done on these topics immediately. Some appear not to have been addressed at all, or at least manuscript drafts did not survive. Several are addressed in essays published after Mill's death (including religion of humanity, utility of religion and socialism) – it is not always clear

---

[32] Mill, Letter 30, to Taylor Mill, after 29 October 1850, *CW* XIV, 49.

[33] I engage at more length with the question of Mill's involvement in Chapter 5.

[34] See Hayek, *John Stuart Mill and Harriet Taylor*, 179. Mill's mother and remaining unmarried sisters did not immediately call on Taylor Mill when told of Mill's engagement. Their reasons are unclear, but it seems to have been a cause of offence for which Mill never forgave them.

[35] Mill, *Statement on Marriage*, 99; Mill, Letter 102, to Taylor Mill, 29 August 1853, *CW* XIV, 110; Mill, Letter 103, to Taylor Mill, 30 August 1853, *CW* XIV, 111.

[36] Mill, Letter 126, to Taylor Mill, 7 February 1854, *CW* XIV, 152.

when Mill started work on them. He wrote a review of George Grote's *Plato* in 1866.[37] (He had already engaged with two publications on Plato in 1840.)[38] His *Utilitarianism* (1861) may also be an outcome of a desire to write on the '[f]oundation of morals'. 'Family' is at least partially tackled in *Subjection of Women*, which was published in 1869, though first written in 1860.[39]

Of all the proposed topics, liberty is the one most closely associated with Mill. He went on a long journey to Italy in the winter of 1854–5 for his health, where he was inspired to restart work on the essay which would become *On Liberty*.[40] On his return, he recalls that he and Taylor Mill worked on the manuscript together, going through every sentence in collaboration as co-authors.[41] The manuscript was with them when they started a journey to warmer climes together in autumn 1858. Tragically, at Avignon, Taylor Mill was overcome by a massive haemorrhage, and died on 3 November 1858. *On Liberty* was published in February 1859. The dedication reads:

> To the beloved and deplored memory of her who was the inspirer, and in part the author of, all that is best in my writings – the friend and wife whose exalted sense of truth and right was my strongest incitement, and whose approbation was my chief reward – I dedicate this volume. Like all that I have written for many years, it belongs as much to her as to me. ... Were I but capable of interpreting to the world one half of the great thoughts and noble feelings which are buried in her grave, I should be the medium of a greater benefit to it, than is ever likely to arise from anything that I can write, unprompted and unassisted by her all but unrivalled wisdom.[42]

Taylor Mill was buried in Avignon, under a gravestone of Carrera marble Mill had especially imported. Mill bought a house near the graveyard, and lived there for several months of each year, even when he was an MP (1865–8). He died on 7 May 1873, and is buried in the same grave.

Some of Mill's most famous works (including *Utilitarianism*, *Subjection of Women* and *Considerations on Representative Government*) were published in the decade after Taylor Mill's death. However, properly understanding their close, collaborative relationship (not least, long and deep conversations over almost their whole adult lives) means we should recognise Taylor Mill contributed even to books published posthumously. (This also includes Mill's *Autobiography*, which was published after they had both died.)

Taylor Mill's role in Mill's life, and work, was recognised by some contemporaries, with obituaries including reference to the fact that Mill had, '[d]uring

---

[37] Mill, *Grote's Plato*, 375–440.   [38] Mill, *Two Publications on Plato*, 239–43.
[39] See Collini, 'Introduction', xxxii.
[40] Mill, Letter 213, to Taylor Mill, 15 January 1855, *CW* XIV, 294.
[41] Mill, *Autobiography*, 257–9.   [42] Mill, *On Liberty*, 216.

more than twenty years ... been aided by her talents and encouraged by her sympathy in all the work he had undertaken'; that, after their marriage, 'never did a philosopher find a more devoted or absorbing companion'; and that 'she must have been gifted with the rarest powers of moral and intellectual sympathy, for she awoke in Mill an admiration as passionate as it was pure'.[43]

Over the years, however, her own contributions to political thought have tended to be forgotten (as is so often the case with female writers), and her contributions to 'Mill's' work have been denied, denigrated or downplayed. She has variously been cast as a vain self-aggrandiser, a self-appointed 'goddess' demanding worship and fealty, and a neurotic woman obsessed with violence.[44] The consensus (by, generally, but by no means exclusively, male writers) seems to have been that both she and Mill had a greatly exaggerated view of her abilities and her contribution, and she could safely be consigned to the dustbin of history – a rather embarrassing aberration on Mill's part, his otherwise clear sight being at least partially blinded by love.[45]

In more recent years, there has been an effort to re-evaluate Taylor Mill as a thinker in her own right, and as a co-author with her more famous second husband.[46] This was begun by Friedrich Hayek, in 1951, with his *John Stuart Mill and Harriet Taylor: Their Friendship and Subsequent Marriage*, added to by Alice Rossi's bringing together of Mill and Taylor Mill's *Essays on Sex Equality* in 1970, and greatly extended by Jo-Ellen Jacobs' production of *Complete Works of Harriet Taylor Mill* in 1998. Taylor Mill was included in the *Stanford Encyclopaedia of Philosophy* in 2002,[47] and as one of the *Philosopher Queens* in the book of that name in 2020.[48] In the rest of this Element I will explore some of the key themes of her work.

2 Liberty, Individuality and Toleration

Questions around freedom were central to Harriet Taylor Mill's work from her earliest writings through literally to her death – according to John Stuart Mill, the manuscript of *On Liberty* was with them when she died. *On Liberty* is perhaps Mill's most famous book, featuring not only on thousands of student reading lists but are also cited in much public discourse around free speech and freedom of thought, conscience and action. The dedication (read by many every year, but not generally taken too seriously) is '[t]o the beloved and

---

[43] See Jacobs, 'The Lot of Gifted Ladies Is Hard', 132–62.
[44] See McCabe, *John Stuart Mill, Socialist*, 249–55.
[45] See, for instance, Crisp, *Routledge Philosophy Guidebook to Mill on Utilitarianism*, 5.
[46] On this, see Phillips, 'The "Beloved and Deplored" Memory of Harriet Taylor Mill', 626–42.
[47] See Miller, 'Harriet Taylor'.   [48] See McCabe, 'Harriet Taylor' in *The Philosopher Queens*.

deplored memory of her who was the inspirer, and in part the author, of all that is best in my writings', his 'friend and wife', Taylor Mill.[49] 'Like all that I have written for many years', Mill added, 'it belongs as much to her as to me'.

Although Taylor Mill has sometimes been cast as more 'socialist', and – by inference – more authoritarian than Mill, she was actually an ardent champion of individual freedom, diversity and, as *On Liberty* puts it, 'the free development of individuality'.[50] The core themes of *On Liberty* – toleration of difference, and letting people act as they see fit so long as they do not cause harm to others; freedom of thought and speech; the dangers of social control and homogeneity; and championing diversity as central to individual well-being and social progress – are to be found in Taylor Mill's writings throughout her life.

Toleration was one of her earliest concerns. In a piece written on paper watermarked 1832 but otherwise undatable, Taylor Mill noted that 'toleration' had not improved much since the sixteenth century: 'Our faults of uncharitableness have rather changed their objects than their degree. The root of all intolerance, the spirit of conformity, remains; and not until that is destroyed, will envy hatred and all uncharitableness, with their attendant hypocrisies, be destroyed too'.[51]

This said, she was sceptical of toleration as anything but a 'negative' virtue.[52] '[W]ere the spirit of toleration abroad', she wrote, 'the name of toleration would be unknown'. That is, if we were actually and actively tolerant, the idea of 'toleration' would not be necessary. '[T]o tolerate', she said, 'is to abstain from unjust interference'. This is a good thing, and already rare in contemporary society where people might not lie or slander, but they certainly did not mind 'evil speaking', and where a variety of 'unjust interference[s]' with people's liberty were permitted and even praised.

'[H]ostility to individual character' was, she thought, the 'spirit' at the root of religious, political, social and moral conformity. This collective hostility was so strong that, on the rare occasions that individual character was developed, it was forced to remain secret. She used the metaphor of the Ancient Roman 'fasces' – a bundle of rods with a projecting axe head, which symbolised the magistrate's power – to explain this power. '[T]he indolent minded many' had raised a 'standard of conformity' which was 'guarded by a fasces of opinion which, though composed individually of the weakest of twigs, yet makes up collectively a mass which is not to be resisted with impunity'. Individually, a 'weak' or 'mentally listless' person could not oppose the 'strong' or 'mental[ly]

---

[49] Mill, *On Liberty*, 216.   [50] *Ibid.*, 261.   [51] Taylor Mill, *Complete Works*, 137.
[52] *Ibid.*, 139.

independent' – but society was made up of 'many' weak, and only a 'few' strong, and collectively the weak could prevent the self-development of almost everyone, forcing them to conform.

Taylor Mill criticised the 'propriety-ridden' nature of the English, with the aim of so many not being their own happiness, nor that of any particular other, but 'to attain some standard of right or duty erected by some or other of the sets into which society is divided'.[53] With one of her frequent flashes of humour and eye for a memorable metaphor, she likens these divisions to 'a net to catch gudgeons'.[54]

We see here Taylor Mill's long-standing commitment to individuality. Rather than forced conformity, she wanted freedom, and rather than 'negative' toleration she ideally wanted a more 'positive' championing of, and love for, difference and 'the free development of individuality'.[55] Here, too, we see a foreshadowing of *On Liberty*'s emphasis on the need for 'active' rather than 'passive' minds and personalities, and its championing of the kind of atmosphere needed for individual character to flourish.[56] We see, too, a clear link with the critique of contemporary society given in *On Liberty* that

> [T]he man, and still more the woman, who can be accused either of doing 'what nobody does' or of not doing 'what everybody does', is the subject of as much depreciatory remark as if he or she had committed some grave moral delinquency.[57]

Rather than seeing acting differently to how contemporary social mores dictated as 'immoral', Taylor Mill argued that eccentric people were more likely to be 'principle[d]' than those who, though often *called* principled, were, in her eyes, merely 'the slaves of some dicta or other', unable to think or act for themselves.[58] (Again, this is very reminiscent of arguments found later in *On Liberty*.[59])

Taylor Mill's response to the pressures of conformity was to exhort people to 'think for yourself, and act for yourself', and she called for everyone to be made 'strong enough to stand alone' for 'whoever has known the pleasure of self-dependence, will be in no danger of relapsing into subserviency'.[60] She had what we might now think was an overly optimistic belief that once people saw that the social, political and religious mores which ruled them were a 'phantom', they would 'cease to be led altogether' and 'each mind' would 'guide itself by the light of as much knowledge as it can acquire for itself by means of unbiased

---

[53] *Ibid.*, 138. See Mill and Taylor-Mill, *On Liberty*, 264–5.
[54] Taylor Mill, *Complete Works*, 138.   [55] Mill and Taylor-Mill, *On Liberty*, 261.
[56] *Ibid.*, 242, 262–6.   [57] *Ibid.*   [58] *Ibid.*, 264.   [59] *Ibid.*, 260–75.
[60] Taylor Mill, *Complete Works*, 138.

opinion'. Even if people did *not* have the strength to think or act for themselves, she added, they should, at the very least, 'attempt not to impede, much less to resent the genuine expression of . . . others'.

A 'positive' toleration, then, would not impede people's attempt to think and act for themselves, and would also not 'resent' the genuine expression of people's individuality, instead looking kindly on diversity, difference and eccentricity. Indeed, a whole chapter of *On Liberty* explains how 'the free development of individuality' is a key element of well-being.[61] This freedom benefits not just those who develop their own individuality but everyone else in society who can learn from their (good or bad) example. In a famous passage, Taylor Mill and Mill explain how:

> As it is useful that while mankind are imperfect there should be different opinions, so is it that there should be different experiments of living; that free scope should be given to varieties of character, short of injury to others; and that the worth of different modes of life should be proved practically, when any one thinks fit to try them. It is desirable, in short, that in things which do not primarily concern others, individuality should assert itself. Where, not the person's own character, but the traditions or customs of other people are the rule of conduct, there is wanting one of the principal ingredients of human happiness, and quite the chief ingredient of individual and social progress.[62]

Mill and Taylor Mill made a similar argument more than ten years before the publication of *On Liberty*, in *Principles of Political Economy*, where they wrote of communism that '[t]he question is, whether there would be any asylum left for individuality of character' or 'whether public opinion would ... be a tyrannical yoke' and the communist system 'grind all down into a tame uniformity of thoughts, feelings, and actions'.[63] They added:

> This is already one of the glaring evils of the existing state of society, notwith-standing a much greater diversity of education and pursuits. ... No society in which eccentricity is a matter of reproach, can be in a wholesome state. It is yet to be ascertained whether the Communistic scheme would be consistent with that multiform development of human nature, those manifold unlikeness, that diversity of tastes and talents, and variety of intellectual points of view, which not only form a great part of the interest of human life, but by bringing intellects into stimulating collision, and by presenting to each innumerable notions that he would not have conceived of himself, are the mainspring of mental and moral progression.

---

[61] See Mill and Taylor-Mill, *On Liberty*, 260–75. [62] *Ibid.*, 260–1.
[63] Mill, *Principles of Political Economy*, 209. Mill said in his *Autobiography* (255–7) that Taylor Mill had a 'conspicuous' part in his treatment of various socialist schemes (including commun-ism) in *Principles*, meaning we can plausibly consider her a co-author of these sections.

Individuality is a word which is often linked to individualism, but which is used in *On Liberty* to mean our unique character – that which makes us 'individual' or dissimilar from all other human beings in the world. It was something of primary concern to Taylor Mill as early as the 1830s, and throughout her life, as the aforementioned quotes show. Well over a decade before even this passage from *Principles* was written, Taylor Mill wrote of how

> [W]omen ... are entirely deprived of all those advantages of academical or university instruction[,] emulation & example which are open to all men: and what is much more important to the formation or development of individuality of character, the whole repute of their lives is made to depend on their utter exclusion from any source of knowledge or experience of the world – and the varieties of scene & of character which must be known and tried to give self-knowledge, and decision of mind.[64]

This passage may reflect Taylor Mill's own frustrations as an intelligent woman denied opportunities for formal education, access to meaningful work outside the home and the freedom to develop her own character and live according to her own lights. But as Hayek rightly notes, her own experiences 'were by no means the limit of her rationalist revolt against the tyranny of public opinion'.[65]

Her argument here is strikingly similar to that of *On Liberty*, though there it is no longer gender specific, and the need for both men and women to have experience of 'varieties ... of character', and the opportunity to 'know and tr[y]' them in order to achieve 'self-knowledge, and decision of mind' is asserted and defended.[66] There, too, Wilhelm Von Humboldt's phrase (from 1854) that 'individuality of power and development' requires 'freedom, and variety of situations' is quoted (in translation).[67] Mill and Taylor Mill added:

> [I]t is the privilege and proper condition of a human being, arrived at the maturity of his faculties, to use and interpret experience in his own way. It is for him to find out what part of recorded experience is properly applicable to his own circumstances and character ... to educate ... [and] develop in him[self] ... the qualities which are the distinctive endowment of a human being. The human faculties of perception, judgement, discriminative feeling, mental activity, and even moral preference, are exercised only in making a choice. ... He who chooses his plan for himself, employs all his faculties. He must use observation to see, reasoning and judgement to foresee, activity to gather materials for decision, discrimination to decide,

---

[64] Taylor Mill, *Complete Works*, 5–6.   [65] Hayek, *John Stuart Mill and Harriet Taylor*, 25–6.
[66] Mill and Taylor-Mill, *On Liberty*, 260–75.
[67] *Ibid.* Mill's footnote is to *The Sphere and Duties of Government*, from the German of Baron Wilhelm von Humboldt, 11 and 13. This is from the English translation by Joseph Coulthard (John Chapman, 1854).

and when he has decided, firmness and self-control to hold to his deliberate decision.[68]

This belief was central to Taylor Mill's political philosophy, right from when she first started writing about individual liberty and happiness through to her death. She uses 'individuality' in the way it is used in *On Liberty* much earlier than she and Mill had read it in von Humboldt, and, indeed, somewhat earlier than there is evidence of Mill himself using it, and this central idea of *On Liberty* was evidently something very close to her heart.[69]

As well as being famous for its championing of the importance for happiness of 'the free development of individuality', and the need for people to be able to make 'experiments of living', *On Liberty* is probably most famous for the 'liberty principle' or 'harm principle' first stated in its opening chapter. This asserts that:

> The sole end for which mankind are warranted, individually or collectively, in interfering with the liberty of action of any of their number is self-protection . . . the only purpose for which power can be rightfully exercised over any member of a civilised community, against his will, is to prevent harm to others.[70]

This principle offers a justification for some interference (preventing harm) as well as the point at which this interference is warranted (when it is necessary to prevent harm to another). As co-author of this principle, so famous and so foundational to liberalism, Taylor Mill deserves a more prominent place in the history of political thought.

Interestingly, this seems to have been an idea she had been wrestling with since at least the 1830s. In a piece from the first half of that decade, she wrote, but then crossed out, 'No government has the right to interfere with . . . personal freedom', and rephrased this as 'Every human being has the right to all personal freedom which does not interfere with the happiness of some other.'[71] This idea contains within it, arguably, the seed of *On Liberty*'s famous harm principle.

The ideas are, of course, expressed differently. In Taylor Mill's early version, interference with personal liberty is permitted only when someone else's happiness is 'interfered' with: in *On Liberty* this has changed to the idea of 'harm'.

---

[68] Mill, *On Liberty*, 263.

[69] The first real evidence is from 1838 when, in *Bentham* (Mill, *Bentham*, 107–8), Mill said 'it is necessary that the institutions of society should make provision for keeping up . . . as . . . a shelter for freedom of thought and individuality of character, a perpetual and standing Opposition'. Mill also wrote, in 1836, that after the French Revolution 'the duties of a citizen . . . demanded the annihilation of every individuality' (Mill, *Guizot's Lectures on European Civilisation*, 384), which is somewhat similar.

[70] Mill and Taylor-Mill, *On Liberty*, 223.   [71] Taylor Mill, *Complete Works*, 19.

However, as both Taylor Mill and Mill were utilitarians, the ideas of (un) happiness and harm are not very far apart.

Utilitarianism has as its base the ethical principle that 'actions are right in proportion as they tend to promote happiness, wrong as they tend to produce the reverse of happiness'.[72] In *On Liberty*, Mill and Taylor Mill wrote:

> I regard utility as the ultimate appeal on all ethical questions: but it must be utility in the largest sense, grounded on the permanent interests of man as a progressive being. Those interests, I contend, authorize the subjection of individual spontaneity to external control, only in respect to those actions of each, which concern the interest of other people.[73]

They added, '[i]n all things which regard the external relations of the individual, he is ... amenable to those whose interests are concerned, and if need be, to society as their protector'.

Harm, then, is something which adversely affects our interests. These interests are closely connected with happiness, because 'utility' is grounded on them. We might recast Taylor Mill's original statement, therefore, as 'every human being has the right to all personal freedom which does not harm some other'. 'Personal freedom' can be mapped onto the realm of activity which does not harm others, as it is in *On Liberty*, combining both what are referred to as 'self-regarding' actions (i.e. those where our own interests are primarily at stake) and some other regarding actions (i.e. those which affect the interests of others but which do not cause harm e.g. voluntary contracts, giving people presents, forming loving relationships).

Taylor Mill was asserting a large scope for personal liberty, and suggesting a prima facie limit (negative interference with the happiness of another). The same is true of *On Liberty*. Both Taylor Mill's early expression and the one we find in *On Liberty* set the boundary in a comparable place, and are keen to assert as wide a field for personal freedom as possible, compatible with other people enjoying the same liberty.

On Liberty can be read as defending (and demanding) that people are 'left alone', and as such aligns with a traditional liberal understanding of freedom as 'lack of constraint'.[74] (The most famous expression is probably Isaiah Berlin's idea of 'negative freedom.'[75]) But the emphasis on 'sovereignty', on the *development* of individuality and on activity point to a concept of liberty that is not *just* the idea that freedom is non-interference. Instead, freedom becomes

---

[72] Mill, *Utilitarianism*, 210.   [73] Mill and Taylor-Mill, *On Liberty*, 224.

[74] For a good summary of the centrality of this idea to liberal thought, see MacGilvray, *Liberal Freedom*, 41–9.

[75] Berlin, 'Two Concepts of Liberty'.

something more like autonomy (in a letter of 1871 Mill himself described his, and Taylor Mill's, notion as 'autonomie'[76]) or 'independence'.[77]

Indeed, in Taylor Mill's writings, particularly on women (and echoed in *Subjection*), we see something of what is often called a 'republican' idea of freedom – which understands liberty as freedom from domination by the arbitrary will of another.[78] This, too, is a central element of the 'independence' or 'sovereignty' which the 'harm principle' would protect.[79]

This concept of freedom ties Taylor Mill's work to that of the earlier feminist, Mary Wollstonecraft, who championed a 'republican' form of liberty.[80] However, as well as emphasising the importance (as do other republicans) of an equality which makes domination impossible, and political and economic participation, Taylor Mill emphasised the need (which republicans do not) of a sphere of non-interference in which we can freely develop our individuality. The 'freedom' there is non-interference as well as non-domination, and the 'development' is something active and self-guided (thus linked to autonomy and 'sovereignty'). Thus, with Mill, Taylor Mill developed a unique, complex and compelling idea of freedom which sets her apart from other liberals, and earlier feminists. (Though, as I will explore later, this emphasis on non-interference did not mean Taylor Mill was an advocate of traditional laissez-faire economic policy, instead advocating a form of socialism in which working people could become independent through the communal ownership of capital.)

Thus, we can see that the ideas which informed *On Liberty* had a long life in both the work, and minds, of Taylor Mill and Mill. Freedom was of great importance to both of them, as is clear not only from their published and unpublished works but also from their including 'liberty' in the list of topics on which they wanted to write in 1854.[81] Their longevity in Taylor Mill's writing adds weight to Mill's assertion that he and Taylor Mill co-authored *On Liberty*.

Recent work by scholars working with digital humanities techniques has shown that 'a lot of *On Liberty* has not been written by J[ohn] S[tuart] M[ill] alone', with strong links between *Enfranchisement*, *Considerations of Representative Government*, *Utilitarianism* and *On Liberty*.[82] Taken with

---

[76] Mill, Letter 1678, to Emile Acollas, 20 September 1871, *CW* XVII, 1832.

[77] See McCabe, *John Stuart Mill, Socialist*, 145–60.

[78] See MacGilvray, *Liberal Freedom*, 52–85.

[79] See McCabe, *John Stuart Mill, Socialist*, 152–3.

[80] For more on Taylor Mill's connections to Wollstonecraft, see McCabe, 'Harriet Taylor' in *The Wollstonecraftian Mind*.

[81] Mill, Letter 126, 152.

[82] Schmidt-Petri, Schefczyk and Osburg, 'Who Authored *On Liberty*?', 120–38.

Mill's own recollections, and what we find in Taylor Mill's manuscripts, this should make us consider *On Liberty* a jointly authored text. In turn, this should challenge notions not only of what women can and have contributed to political philosophy (and the place of Taylor Mill herself in the canon of the history of political thought) but also the way in which we think philosophy is done: it is not solely (if ever) produced by solitary thinkers, but is instead the product of close collaboration, shared thinking, debate and discussion.

In his *Autobiography*, Mill said:

> The *Liberty* is likely to survive longer than anything else that I have written … because the conjunction of her mind with mine has rendered it a kind of philosophic text-book of a single truth, which the changes progressively taking place in modern society tend to bring out into ever strong relief: the importance, to man and society, of a large variety in types of character, and of giving full freedom to human nature to expand itself in innumerable and conflicting directions.[83]

This is also Taylor Mill's legacy when it comes to a core area of political thought, that is, personal liberty and the proper justifications for interference with it by state and society. Her ideas regarding toleration, freedom of speech, freedom of action, and the importance of 'the free development of individuality', are foundational to liberalism. With Mill, she offered new and fruitful arguments on these topics on which we still rely today. Taylor Mill championed the claims and interests of individuals, but was also cognisant of the claims, and needs, of others, and the need to carefully balance one against the other. Her solution was a wide sphere of unlimited freedom, bounded only by consideration for the happiness of others – in her own life, and in her political philosophy.

3 Marriage, Sexual Relationships and Divorce

When mentioned in the history of political thought at all, Harriet Taylor Mill is generally included among 'early', 'first-wave' feminists. Though we should not pigeonhole Taylor Mill as *solely* writing on 'women's issues', she developed a series of interesting arguments regarding women's equality and liberty. She was committed to women's equality long before she met John Stuart Mill, and he recalled that it was his own commitment to this cause which first attracted her to him when they met.[84] Her most famous feminist work is *Enfranchisement of Women*. I will explore this text in more detail in Section 5. Here, I want to consider her feminist analysis of marriage, divorce and the nature of sexual relationships.

---

[83] Mill, *Autobiography*, 259.   [84] *Ibid.*, 253.

Taylor Mill was harshly critical of a society in which marriage was women's only option for security as well as social- and self-respect, and said that the idea 'that the great object of women's life is love' was merely a 'popular fallacy'.[85] This said, she also felt that egalitarian, voluntary interpersonal relationships could be of great importance for personal happiness and was herself deeply in love with at least two men in her lifetime. She was opposed to what she described as 'sensualism', but saw sex of the right kind as one of the highest pleasures. She was committed to the 'perfect equality' of both sexes in society and personal relationships. Linked to her perennial concern with liberty, the central element for Taylor Mill in marriage, sexual relationships and, ultimately, divorce was freedom. People should only be in relationships which both wanted, and to the extent that the state should regulate these matters at all, the aim should be to preserve freedom and independence as much as possible.

Taylor Mill's longest piece directly engaging with these themes is her essay *On Marriage*, written as a pair with one of the same name by Mill. She also engaged with some of these questions in unpublished manuscripts written around the same time as *Enfranchisement* and perhaps initially intended to form a part of it. These manuscripts are also clearly linked to *Subjection of Women* (1869), which Mill initially wrote after Taylor Mill's death at the urging of his stepdaughter (in 1860), and which he said was drawn from a common 'fund of thought' built over many years with Taylor Mill.[86]

Both essays on marriage are undated, but as Taylor Mill cites a poem by Alfred, Lord Tennyson not published until 1833 in an early draft of hers, this seems the likeliest year of composition.[87] Taylor Mill wrote that, in order to 'raise ... the condition of women', the '*purpose*' of any planned reform should be 'to remove all interference with affection, or with anything which is, or which even might be supposed to be, demonstrative of affection'.[88] This was an important goal in itself, as it allowed people essential liberty and the ability to freely develop their individuality,[89] but it also had important implications for individual happiness.[90]

She advocated what would now be called 'no-fault' divorces. 'Would not the best plan', she asked, 'be divorce which could be attained by *any*, *without any reason assigned*, and a small expense ... ?'. However, she thought they should 'only be finally pronounced after a long period', not less than two years, in case

---

[85] Taylor Mill, *Complete Works*, 225.   [86] Mill, *Autobiography*, 265.

[87] Hayek (*John Stuart Mill and Harriet Taylor*, 57) dates the essays slightly earlier, but the evidence from Taylor Mill's puts them both in 1833, and probably before November, when they went to Paris.

[88] Taylor Mill, *Complete Works*, 21.   [89] Mill and Taylor-Mill, *On Liberty*, 261.

[90] Taylor Mill, *Complete Works*, 43–4 (see also *CW* XXI, 387).

people changed their minds.[91] This said, 'what the decision will be *must* be certain at the moment of asking for it, *unless* during that time the suit should be withdrawn'. That is, the waiting period is in case people experience a sort of 'buyer's remorse' – it is not a period of doubt and resultant anxiety about whether a divorce will, in the end, be granted. '500 years hence', she wrote, 'none of the follies of their ancestors will so excite wonder and contempt as the fact of legislative restraint as to matters of feeling – or rather in the expressions of feeling'.[92] Perhaps she was right, though no-fault divorce was only recently made legal in the United Kingdom (and, though she probably did not have these in mind, same-sex relationships, never mind marriages, are still illegal, and very dangerous, in many countries in the world, almost 200 years after she wrote those words).

Taylor Mill defined marriage as 'a legal obligation wh[ich] binds any person to live with, or be dependent on, another, against their inclination – wh[ich] makes the person of one human being the property of another'.[93] She was highlighting how the law made women dependent on men, because marriage meant they no longer had property rights, rights to their own earnings, the right not to have sex with their husbands or the right to leave and live somewhere separately from him. 'Ladies in love', Taylor Mill wrote, might mean and want to live by all that they had sworn in their Christian marriage vows – they had, however, 'no business to undertake to arrange what is right & wrong for other women'.[94] That is, dependency, loss of sexual autonomy and a man determining where you live might be fine when people consented – but the brutality of marriage was revealed once we considered the position of someone who no longer wanted to be married. Men who knew their wives would rather be with someone else could still insist not only on them living with, and doing domestic work for, them but also on sexual relations – and it was this which Taylor Mill felt made women the 'property' of men. (In this, she is part of a wider tradition of early feminists likening marriage to a form of slavery.[95])

Taylor Mill felt that marriage ought to be 'like any other partnership', 'a real contract between equals'.[96] It should be 'dissoluble at pleasure' so long as this was 'during a sufficiently long period'. There should be 'no merging of any of the individual rights of either of the parties to the contract', and a 'special agreement' should cover any 'interests arising out of marriage' (which might involve joint property or responsibilities towards children). The two contracting

---

[91] *Ibid.*, 22–3.   [92] *Ibid.*, 22.   [93] *Ibid.*, 19.   [94] *Ibid.*, 32.
[95] For more on this, see McCabe, 'Political … Civil and Domestic Slavery', 226–43 and Stevenson, *The Woman as Slave*, especially 69–114.
[96] Taylor Mill, *Complete Works*, 25, 50.

parties 'should each possess their own pecuniary means or earnings free from any power of the other'.

At a time when 'coverture' still existed, such that women became the same legal person as their husbands, meaning they had no legal identity (or rights) 'outside' of him (including over property, earnings and access to their own children), this was a radical argument. It was also radical because it framed marriage as a secular contract which should be like other civil contracts, rather than as a special, religious institution which in some way melded people into one unique unit which could never be divided. Nowadays we are more used to the idea of marriage as a civil contract as many people marry in a registry office without any religious ceremony, and divorces are granted by the state. In Taylor Mill's day, however, marriage was predominantly viewed as a religious institution, and could only happen in a religious building.[97]

Although desiring marriage to be a contract, Taylor Mill was critical of the way in which women were deliberately kept in ignorance of what they were agreeing to when they made their marriage vows. Girls' education and social ideas around 'purity' meant that young women 'enter into what is called a contract perfectly ignorant of the conditions of it, and that they should be so is considered absolutely essential to their fitness for it!'.[98] That is, girls marry without full knowledge of the terms and conditions of the marriage contract (hence why she casts doubt on whether we can really call it a contract), and men only think girls who are virgins and know nothing about sex are suitable people with whom to contract a marriage (which puts them in a position of unequal power, as male virginity is not seen as a prerequisite for marriage, indeed often the opposite, which also makes men hypocrites).

As well as highlighting the fact that women could hardly be said to consent to contemporary marriages, Taylor Mill was highly critical of the attitudes of the men who made these contracts, and particularly who insisted on holding women to them. 'Who', she asked, 'would wish to have the person without the inclination?'[99] Perhaps optimistically, she says 'I think no one'.

She wrote that divorce should be called 'proof of affection': that is, if people wanted to stay married, that was proof of their mutual affection – if they did not, then they should be allowed to dissolve their marriage.[100]

Taylor Mill acknowledged that '[a]ll the difficulties about divorce seem to be in the consideration for the children'.[101] Instead of this being an argument against divorce, however, she saw it as an argument for greater equality, and particularly improved education and employment opportunities for women

---

[97] See 1836 (34) Marriages: A Bill for Marriages in England.
[98] Taylor Mill, *Complete Works*, 23.   [99] *Ibid.*   [100] *Ibid.*, 23.   [101] *Ibid.*

(and the right to their own earnings). If women could be financially independent, and knew they might have to support any children they had, she felt they would be less likely to have children in the first place: they would not need them as a 'tie' to their husband (preserving their marriage, and themselves from being abandoned), and they would be cautious about the burden children would place on their own financial position.

Indeed, to the extent that marriage engenders dependence in women and gives men great power over them, as well as limiting the freedom of both parties, Taylor Mill wrote, 'I have no doubt that when the whole community is really educated, tho' the present laws of marriage were to continue they would be perfectly disregarded because no one would marry.'[102] Her preferred solution, though, was not this, but 'placing women on the most entire equality with men, as to all rights and privileges, civil and political, and then doing away with all laws whatever relating to marriage'.[103] In such a world jobs and opportunities would be equally open to all, and '[f]athers would provide for their daughters in the same manner as for their sons'. Thus, '[w]omen would have no more reason to barter person for bread … than men have' in contemporary society.

Taylor Mill's view was somewhat more radical than Mill's (as expressed in his *On Marriage*), who had rather conservative concerns about divorce allowing people to too frequently change partners and thus never persevere with a relationship, leading to general discontent and unhappiness.[104] Though offering no reasons for his view, he said it was 'desirable that the first choice should be, even if not compulsorily, yet very generally, persevered in'.[105] He also asserted that children '*must* be better cared for … if their parents remain together'. However, he also felt that the weight of all the arguments against divorce 'is not so great as it appears', and, like Taylor Mill, supported no-fault divorces which were easily obtainable.[106]

In an undated manuscript, Taylor Mill also wrote:

> Divorce is more needed by women than men by all the difference between having <u>none</u> & having <u>all</u> the power. It is no answer to say that no man who is either a good man or a gentleman takes advantage of the unjust power the law gives him; what injustice is there which human beings will not commit when tempted by passion, even when they know they are wrong, how much more

---

[102] *Ibid.*, 22.　　[103] *Ibid.*, 23.

[104] Mill, *On Marriage*, 45–9. Mill later criticised Auguste Comte for his concern that 'liberty of divorce' would lead to 'a constant succession of experiments and failures', saying experience shows such a 'succession' is 'inconsistent' with 'modern habits and feelings' (Mill, *Auguste Comte and Positivism*, 311). This suggests Mill changed his mind on this argument against divorce between 1833 and 1865.

[105] Mill, *On Marriage*, 46.　　[106] *Ibid.*, 48.

when law & custom tell them they are right! But even if it could be granted that no good man & no gentleman would take advantage of his power to tyrannise, how many men of any bodys [*sic*] acquaintance are in the christian [*sic*] sense good men ... ? But if they were both to depend on the forbearance of another is not a healthy or just state of human relations.[107]

This passage has strong echoes of the arguments in *Subjection*, where – however – the argument is more generally for women's equality in marriage, not overtly for divorce.[108] Such passages are a reminder that *Subjection*, too, was influenced by Taylor Mill and should not be seen as solely Mill's work.

Mill and Taylor Mill also treated publicly with the question of divorce in *On Liberty*, written just before Taylor Mill's death. Her last word on the subject, then, is that, in general, the 'liberty principle' 'requires that those who have become bound to one another, in things which concern no third party, should be able to release each other from the engagement', and that no contracts, save perhaps those relating to money, are entirely indissoluble.[109] Marriage, though, is a special case, and it should be harder to dissolve than some other contracts, morally speaking at least, even if not legally, particularly if there are children.

Though they praised him elsewhere, she and Mill argued that von Humboldt's arguments for divorce were based on too 'simple' 'grounds': something 'more than the declared will of either party' must be needed to dissolve a marriage. (Von Humboldt's arguments as parsed in *On Liberty* are similar to those of Taylor Mill's *On Marriage*, showing her view developed over time, perhaps due to reflection on her own circumstances.) Taylor Mill and Mill bring in a new argument against complete liberty of divorce: that in divorcing someone we may wrong them by destroying 'expectations and calculations' which they legitimately formed based on our 'express promise or ... conduct'. From such promises and conduct 'a new series of moral obligations arises ... towards that person, which may possibly be overruled, but cannot be ignored'.

This new argument is entirely in keeping with their utilitarianism. That is, as utilitarians, and particularly as utilitarians who put emphasis on the importance of security, Mill and Taylor Mill thought that new obligations arose from our (implicitly or explicitly) allowing people to build their lives on certain expectations of our future behaviour. This was even more the case if people had had children, where 'obligations arise on the part of both the contracting parties ... the fulfilment of which, or at all events the mode of fulfilment, must be greatly

---

[107] Taylor Mill, *Complete Works*, 24.

[108] Mill, *Subjection of Women*, 287–90. For more on Mill's views on divorce (and their link to Bentham), see Mill, *Whewell on Moral Philosophy*, 198–9 and Mill, *Auguste Comte and Positivism*, 311.

[109] Mill and Taylor-Mill, *On Liberty*, 300.

affected by the continuance or disruption of the relation between the original parties to the contract'.

This said, they were keen to assert that '[i]t does not follow ... that these obligations extend to requiring the fulfilment of the contract at all costs to the happiness of the reluctant party', though they were 'a necessary element in the question'. These considerations 'ought not to make *much* difference' 'in the *legal* freedom of the parties to release themselves from the engagement' but 'they necessarily make a great difference in the *moral* freedom'.[110] Taylor Mill and Mill insisted that people ought to 'take all these circumstances into account' before determining on divorce (and that someone who did not would be 'morally responsible for the wrong' done to the 'reluctant party' and any children). However, they still favoured (though without saying it overtly) the legal availability of 'no-fault' divorces, and also emphasised that the question of divorce was 'usually discussed as if the interest of children was everything, and that of grown persons nothing', an attitude of which they evidently disapproved. (And which reflects Taylor Mill's attitude from 1833 more than Mill's.)

As well as showing the influence of Taylor Mill's ideas in *On Liberty*, these passages show that her attitude became somewhat more conservative over her lifetime. This said, it is worth noting that even the more cautious passages of *On Liberty* were extremely radical for their day. Both Mill and Taylor Mill may have been reticent to say much in public on this topic, even when this was a subject of significant debate in the 1850s (a Royal Commission recommended the transferral of divorce proceedings from Parliament to a special court in 1853, and the Matrimonial Causes Act was passed in 1857), because of their own personal history, with anything they said being taken to potentially have bearing on Taylor Mill's first marriage.

As well as being intimately linked to freedom, divorce, and a general lack of 'interference' in personal relationships, was, for Taylor Mill, strongly con- nected to increasing happiness. In part this is because of the intimate link between freedom, individuality and well-being (made more plainly in *On Liberty*). However, Taylor Mill also argued that, though it was currently true that 'all the pleasures ... are being men's, and all the disagreeables [*sic*] and pains being women's' in marriage, it was equally certain that the 'pleasure would be infinitely heightened both in kind and degree by the perfect equality of the sexes'.[111]

One reason she gave was that equality would lead to more chance of 'real sympathy or enjoyment of companionship between' married people. At present, Taylor Mill thought, '[w]omen are educated for one single object, to gain their

---

[110] *Ibid.*, 301.   [111] Taylor Mill, *Complete Works*, 24.

living by marrying' or, more bluntly, by making themselves appear sexually attractive to a man. 'The woman', Taylor Mill continued, 'knows what her power is [i.e. sexual attractiveness] and gains by it what she has been taught to consider "proper" to her state'.[112] Women might, Taylor Mill posited, actually ask for much more, but 'their minds are degenerated by habits of dependence'. This led to bad exercises of power by people ill-equipped to exercise power at all (and Taylor Mill critiqued real-world examples of this in the 1830s, 1840s and 1850s). 'Perfect equality' would therefore improve exercises of power, likely leading to less tyranny, pain and unhappiness, and to greater harmony between married people. (This also foreshadows arguments in *Subjection*.)

This said, it is worth emphasising that Taylor Mill had little patience with those who thought women 'should be, not slaves, nor servants, but companions' for men 'and educated for that office'.[113] (She noted that it was never argued that men should be educated to be the companions of women.) These 'moderate reformers' felt that 'cultivated men ... wish ... that his companion should sympathise with him' in his interests 'outside the family circle', and therefore said 'let women improve their understanding and taste, acquire general knowledge, cultivate poetry, art, even coquet with science and ... inform themselves on politics' to the degree where they 'are ... capable of holding a conversation on them with the husband, or at least of understanding and imbibing his wisdom'.[114] This would be, she said, '[v]ery agreeable to him, but unfortunately the reverse of improving', because when men have 'intellectual communion only with those to whom they can lay down the law', they fail 'to advance in wisdom beyond the first stages'. What *is* (or would be) improving 'is communion between active minds, not mere contact between an active mind and a passive'. If 'education took the same pains to form strong-minded women which it takes to prevent them from being formed', then this 'inestimable advantage' would be enjoyed by married couples, to the improvement of both them and society at large.

As well as thinking that a real 'companionship' might be possible between men and women if education was reformed, Taylor Mill also seems to have thought that sex would be better when people were equals. Taylor Mill was opposed to what she called 'sensualism', but not to sex per se.[115]

'Sensualists' take 'sense' (or the pleasure derived from our senses) 'as the end instead of the means' to pleasure, she wrote.[116] That is, they focus on their own pleasurable physical sensations as the 'end' of pleasure-seeking activity, rather than seeing it as a 'means' to further happiness. (At the extreme, this can

---

[112] *Ibid.*, 22. [113] *Ibid.*, 65 (see also *CW* XXI, 408–9). [114] *Ibid.*, 65–6. [115] *Ibid.*, 19.
[116] *Ibid.*, 18.

lead them to engage in non-consensual sex.) Sensualism, though, does not 'give any pleasure which could not be obtained by higher means', and 'always stand[s] in the way of improvement and the attainment of all that is ... good'. Thus, it is bad for two important reasons.

Taylor Mill was not, however, opposed to a better, 'higher', consensual and more emotional form of sex, where personal sensual pleasure was pursued as a means to an end (the pleasure of others, or strengthening an emotional bond, for instance). Instead, she wrote: '*Sex* in its true and finest meaning, seems to be the way which is manifested all that is highest best and beautiful in the nature of human beings.'[117]

Taylor Mill closely identified pursing the greatest happiness of all, of which an important part was the greatest happiness of one's self, consistent with the greatest happiness of others, with living a virtuous life.[118] Thus, '[w]ho enjoys most, is most virtuous'.[119] This 'most', though, does not apply solely to quantity. Taylor Mill adds, 'the higher the kind of enjoyment, the greater the degree'.[120] (The idea of 'higher' pleasures returns in Mill's *Utilitarianism* as I will discuss in Section 7.) Thus, a certain *kind* of sex – sex enjoyed the right way, where the enjoyment of one's own physical pleasure was not the end, but only a means towards an end – was, for Taylor Mill, a 'higher' pleasure, and was something morally positive and worth pursuing.

This said, Taylor Mill also appears to have disagreed with the idea that 'the exercise of the sexual functions is in any degree a necessity' – instead, she argued, '[i]t is a matter of education'.[121] On the other hand, she also argued (in the same piece) that the idea that 'sensuality is in itself unworthy' was wrong. Instead, she said, '[i]t takes its colour wholly from the individual'. That is, enjoying sensations we experience through our five senses is not necessarily bad, so long as we don't see that as the end of enjoyment, but, instead, are inspired by those pleasurable sensations to other, more emotional or imaginative, pleasures. Moreover, she denied that 'chastity is in itself a virtue', instead believing that '[i]t is neither virtuous nor vicious'. She was not, then, opposed to sex, but to certain attitudes towards it, and modes of engaging in it.

Taylor Mill denied that 'the great object of women's life is love', but this is not to say she did not think love could be an important part of a woman's – or a man's – happiness. For herself, she frequently told Mill of her love, and of the pleasure knowing she was loved by Mill brought her, reassuring him, for instance, that:

> I am loved as I desire to be – heart & soul take their rest in the peace of ample satisfaction ... O my own love, whatever it may or may not be to you,

[117] *Ibid.*, 23.   [118] *Ibid.*, 13.   [119] *Ibid.*, 23–4.   [120] *Ibid.*, 24.   [121] *Ibid.*, 226.

you need never regret for a moment what has already brought such increase of happiness.[122]

What she opposed was the idea that there should *only* be love in women's lives, that their lives were not worth living if they did not find a man to love and, more importantly, marry them and/or if they did not have children to love. Women could find fulfilment and happiness in a variety of other ways, and society ought to be constructed to allow and support them to do so.

Similarly, she denied that 'the chief objects & enjoyments in the life of Mankind are & should be the legalised propagation of the species & the education of their young'.[123] But this does not mean she did not value intimate relationships, or her time spent educating her daughter, with whom she always had a very close relationship, and whom she encouraged in her 'experimental life' as an actress.[124]

We should not think of Taylor Mill, then, as 'anti-sex' or opposed to intimate relationships. Rather the opposite – she thought loving, sexual relationships were of great importance to happiness (though not necessarily for everyone), but only if they were consensual, and between equals. She might not be as 'sex positive' as more modern feminists, in that some sex which they might approve of she might have thought of as 'sensualist', though it is not necessarily true that all short-term relationships need necessarily be 'sensualist' in the bad sense, or that masturbation is necessarily solely 'sensualist'. She was far less prejudiced against sex workers than most women (and men) in her time, saying that women are educated 'to gain their living by marrying – (some poor souls get it without the churchgoing in the same way – they do not seem to me a bit worse than their honoured sisters)',[125] though she was angered that the widespread use of the services of sex workers by men caused so little 'disgust' in society.[126] As her goal was that women would cease to earn their living through marrying, it might well be that she thought they should not earn it through sex work either, in an ideal future. (Similarly, in her ideal world demand for sex workers might dry up, to the extent that it is driven by what she would call the wrong sort of sensualism.)

Taylor Mill's feminism was, then, founded on utility, on liberty and on a strong commitment to egalitarianism, and particularly to equal relationships between people (particularly, though not solely, people in intimate relationships). Her ideal society might have no formal – in particular, legal – rules governing marriage, but it would certainly have loving, committed, intimate relationships. In this, she foreshadows other, more modern, liberal arguments for there being no state-sanctioned marriage laws.[127] What is more, she recognised that to achieve her ideal society there would need to be significant

---

[122] *Ibid.*, 324. [123] *Ibid.*, 225. [124] *Ibid.*, 518. [125] *Ibid.*, 22. [126] *Ibid.*, 13.
[127] See, for instance, Chambers, *Against Marriage*.

economic, political and social changes: women would have to be able to be economically independent from men and able to support a family on their own if necessary; women's education would therefore need to be radically overhauled and improved; daughters should be treated in the same ways as sons, not least when it came to the division of property; and men (and women) would have to look for something rather different in their intimate relationships than they did at present – an equal, not either a dependent or someone on whom to depend.

Political equality was also necessary, and Taylor Mill was a long-standing campaigner for women's suffrage. Responding to potential critics, and their argument against votes for women, that '[y]ou would have perpetual domestic discussion', she responded:

> If people cannot differ in opinion on any important matter and remain capable of living together without quarrelling, there cannot be a more complete condemnation of marriage: for if so, two people cannot live together at all unless one of them is a mere cipher, abdicating all will and opinion into the hands of the other, and marriage can only be fit for tyrants and nobodies.[128]

Instead of this, she had a vision of love between equals – and between equals who were able to freely develop their individuality, and thus be 'somebody' not 'nobody', even if not in any way famous, and who were fully capable of exercising their 'will', even to the extent, if needs be, of demanding a divorce. As well as being central to her philosophy, this was something she fought for, and may have found, in her own life, describing her relationship with Mill as 'the love of two equals'.[129]

Her central commitment to liberty, then, as well as to equality, shaped her views on marriage and on the necessity of divorce. Although she may have become somewhat more conservative as regards the moral permissibility of some divorces in later life, she was always committed to the need for legal no-fault divorces which were easily attainable. She valued intimate personal relationships in her own life, but denied that they were necessarily the be-all and end-all of anyone's (and particularly of women's) happiness. Instead, people ought to be able to freely develop their individuality, pursing their own happiness in their own way (so long as they did not harm others), which might or might not involve sex, marriage and parenthood, and society ought to value all their choices.

4 Gender and Patriarchy

Although an idea more commonly associated with second-wave feminism, several earlier ('first-wave') feminists identified that gender was a social

---

[128] Taylor Mill, *Complete Works*, 40 (see also *CW* XXI, 383).   [129] *Ibid.*, 332–3.

construct, Harriet Taylor Mill among them. Some of her earliest writings criticise the education of women, making them fit for only certain social roles (most obviously, being wives and mothers). She was convinced this was bad for women, but she also argued that it was bad for men. She identified the violence which arose from the patriarchy, enacted both by men over women and by women over those rendered weaker than themselves by inequalities of age and/ or socio-economic position, as well as identifying a number of more invidious ways in which patriarchal power structures oppressed people.

Taylor Mill identified 'the false state in which women stand with regard to the rest of the community' in one of her earliest works: 'All that has yet been said respecting the social condition of women goes on the assumption of their inferiority', she declared.[130] She demanded a 'thorough reform' rather than partial amelioration of women's 'degred[ation]'. As she pointed out, '[w]e hear nothing of the proper influence [of] men, the social rank of men – because that is established', whereas the position of women, except as inferiors, is not. Men, that is, are the 'norm' from which women are the 'other'; men's position in society is taken as given, women always have to make, and are seen as, a special case.

Even radical men 'unthinkingly' cling to their 'belief' in the 'natural inferiority of women', something which she said was 'a lamentable instance of the strength of habits and opinions', thus emphasising that women were not *naturally* unequal, but only made so by social institutions, including the beliefs of both men and many women (which, in turn, are themselves inculcated and reinforced by social institutions such as the family, the church and education). Similarly, 'the end always talked of is always happiness or pleasure to men'.[131] Even when the question is of women's education and women's social and economic position, men are treated as the important beings, whose happiness is to be considered – and their happiness appears to be given more weight, against both the unhappiness and happiness of women. 'We hear nought ... in disquisition on men's education of what sort of instruction will produce the greatest happiness [for] women. We hear no profession of the act of making women happy', but if we are concerned with 'the greatest happiness of all', the 'greatest happiness of each' has to include women. That it does not, in popular (and even in radical, utilitarian) discourse, shows how men are favoured, and women consigned not only to a secondary role in society but also to secondary consideration.

Taylor Mill consistently traces a long history of women's subordination by men (which is also reflected in *Subjection*), and shows how their position has

---

[130] *Ibid.*, 5. [131] *Ibid.*, 7.

gradually improved as physical force (in which men will always, on average, outperform women) has become less and less the sole arbiter of authority.[132] But progress was slow. As she said, 'where ten steps will reach the goal, nine steps take us half way' – much had improved for women, but the final step was to make them, and make men see them as, equals, and not merely 'ministrants to the pleasures of men', and this was a step it seemed men, and society at large, were unwilling to take.[133] Men have 'all the power', and women 'none'.[134] That men do not always *use* all the power they have at their disposal does not make this situation permissible or acceptable – 'to depend on the forbearance of another is not a healthy or just state of human relations'.

In this, Taylor Mill is identifying what we would now call the patriarchy. She was not the first to do this, but her insights are still interesting and important (not least in the history of the development of feminist ideas). She put her finger very neatly on the heart of the problem in *Enfranchisement*:

> The real question is, whether it is right and expedient that one-half of the human race should pass through life in a state of forced subordination to the other half. If the best state of human society is that of being divided into two parts, one consisting of persons with a will and a substantive experience, and the other of humble companions to these persons, attached, each of them to one, for the purpose of bringing up *his* children, and making *his* home pleasant to him . . . is the place assigned to women, it is but kindness to educate them for this. . . . When, however, we ask why the existence of one-half the species should be merely ancillary to that of the other – why each woman should be a mere appendage to a man, allowed to have no interest of her own, that there may be nothing to compete in her mind with his interests and his pleasure; the only reason which can be given is, that men like it. It is agreeable to them that men should live for their own sake, women for the sake of men.[135]

It is in men's interest to keep women in a subordinate position, for women's education 'to make them believe that the greatest good fortune which can befall them is to be chosen by some man' as a wife, and for 'every other career which the world deems happy and honourable' to 'be closed to them by the law' – more, for women to believe this is not just a man-made, 'social' law but a reflection of the immutable laws of 'nature and destiny'. And because it is in men's interest, and because men have pretty much all the power, the situation does not change.

This said, Taylor Mill had some hope for the future. She noted that:

> A great number of progressive changes are constantly going forward in human affairs and ideas, which escape the notice of unreflecting people, because of their slowness. As each successive step requires a whole

---

[132] *Ibid.*, 6, 20, 44, 63–4.   [133] *Ibid.*, 7.   [134] *Ibid.*, 24.   [135] *Ibid.*, 62.

generation or several generations to effect it, and is then only one step, things in reality very changeable remain a sufficient length of time without perceptible progress, to be, by the majority of contemporaries, mistaken for things permanent and immovable and it is only by looking at a long series of generations that they are seen to be, in reality, always moving, and always in the same direction.

This is remarkably the case with respect to Privileges and Exclusions. In every generation, the bulk of mankind imagine that all privileges and all exclusions, then existing by law or usage, are natural, fit and proper, even necessary. ... But when we take history into view we find that its whole course is a getting rid of privileges and exclusions. ... The fact that any particular exclusion exists and has existed hitherto, is ... no presumption whatever that it ought to exist. We may rather surmise that it is probably a remaining relic of that past state of things, in which privilege and exclusion were the general rule.[136]

One such key 'privilege', leading to a series of 'exclusions', was 'the privilege of sex'. '[T]he civil and political disabilities of women', she argued, had 'no foundation in justice or in the interest of society'.

Women were disadvantaged by, and from, birth – but 'it is the boast of England that if some persons are privileged by birth, at least none are disqualified by it', and this held out some hope for change in women's position. As she wrote in an unpublished draft element of *Enfranchisement*, unmarried women who had their own property were currently exempt from 'domestic subjection', and this showed that it was not 'inherently necessary' that *every* woman be denied independence and autonomy. Indeed:

[T]he time cannot be far off when to hold any human being ... in a state of compulsory obedience to any other human being ... will be acknowledged to be as monstrous an infraction of the rights and dignity of humanity, as slavery is at last, though tardily still.[137]

This said, she pulled no punches in her critique of 'the position of women as society has now made it', saying, 'the evil varies ... from being slowly murdered by continued bodily torture, to being only subdued in spirit and thwarted of all those higher and finer developments of individual character of which personal liberty has in all ages been felt to be the indispensable condition'.

Women were disadvantaged by the law (which had been made by men),[138] and custom (made, and supported, by both men and women). Taylor Mill denied 'the alleged superior adaptation of women to certain occupations, and to men of

---

[136] *Ibid.*, 34. For more on Taylor Mill's view of 'progress' and female equality, see Deutscher, 'When Feminism Is "High" and Ignorance Is "Low"', 136–50.

[137] Taylor Mill, *Complete Works*, 44–5.

[138] A point emphasised in one of Taylor Mill's co-authored pieces with Mill – see 'The Suicide of Sarah Brown', 918.

certain others' existed 'to any thing like the extent that is pretended', and – where it *did* exist – it was 'principally if not wholly the effect of differences in education and in social circumstances, or of physical characteristics by no means peculiar to one or the other sex'.

Here we see Taylor Mill asserting what we would now call the social construction of gender. Unlike some more modern feminists, she seems to have thought there was a biological difference between male and female (though we have no firm evidence as to whether she would have, on consideration, thought these were also social constructs), but she was sure that almost all the apparent differences between men and women were the product of education, not anything 'natural' (however 'natural' some elements of that education, as provided by religion and other social institutions, not just schools, might appear).

This was something she thought from her earliest writings. For instance, in the early 1830s we see her wrestling with these ideas when she wrote:

> Whether nature made a difference in the nature of men and women or not, it seems now that all men, with the exception of a few lofty minded, are sensualist more or less. Women on the contrary are quite exempt from this trait, however it may appear otherwise in the cases of some. It seems strange that it should be so, unless it was meant to be a source of power in demi-civilised states such as the present – or it may not be so – it may be only that the habits of freedom and low indulgence in which boys grow up and the contrary notion of what is called purity in girls may have produced the appearance of difference in natures in the two sexes.[139]

Women, Taylor Mill noted, were 'educated for one single object, to gain their living by marrying. .... To be married is the object of their existence and that object being gained they do really cease to exist as to anything worth calling life or any useful purpose'.[140] Again and again she argued against the prevailing idea that '[t]he proper sphere of women is domestic life', and that this warranted barring them from ever being educated for, or being allowed by law to pursue, other careers or interests.[141]

Women's current education (and lack of opportunities outside of marriage) had detrimental effects for both women and men. Like many early feminists, Taylor Mill was unsparing in criticisms of her own gender, particularly when they pandered to men and traditional views of women's 'proper' place.[142] 'The Lord protect us from our friends!' she said ought to be the response 'by women' to 'the books about women written by women'.[143] The social construction of

---

[139] Taylor Mill, *Complete Works*, 21–2.   [140] *Ibid.*, 22–3.   [141] *Ibid.*, 38.   [142] *Ibid.*, 32–4.
[143] *Ibid.*, 32.

womanhood made women dependent on men, and even where men did not exercise the powers the law gave them, women's characters were still affected, no women wanting to risk offending or angering a man who had so much power over her. Thus, Taylor Mill argued, 'the law establishes' 'the bent' of 'the two characters' (i.e. men and women).[144]

> The woman's whole talent goes into the inducing, persuading, coaxing, caressing, in reality the seducing, capacity. In whatever class of life, the woman gains her object by seducing the man. This makes her character quite unconsciously to herself, petty and paltry.

This gave women some power over men – power they often used for 'paltry advantages',[145] or to bad effect when it came to public policy, inducing men to be less 'public-spirited'. This was not necessarily even conscious. Taylor Mill argued that no one can 'long maintain a higher tone of feeling than that of their favourite society'. In contemporary life this 'favourite society' was often a man's wife, but wives were 'the incarnate spirit of family selfishness' unless she had 'accustomed herself to cultivate feelings of a larger and more generous kind', which – in the current state of women's education – was rare and difficult.[146] Taylor Mill wanted to see a time when this power would not be used at all (and would not need to be used), but in the meantime hoped women might use it to better purpose, though her hopes were slight as women, she felt, had 'minds . . . degenerated by habits of dependence'.[147]

As well as this, the patriarchy meant that women could become tyrants over those weaker than themselves, often as a response to the 'despotic' actions of their husbands, denying them 'free-will' in any other way.[148] In the least bad cases, this resulted in the 'petty' thwarting of other people's wishes and ambitions (with further negative consequences, including the build-up of anger and resentment, unhappiness and estrangements between family members); in the worst cases, it led to murder.[149]

Taylor Mill urged men to be aware of this, and change women's conditions – for their own good, if they would not be motivated by a sense of justice towards women. 'Would that men saw how infallibly the mental frustration of the guide of his children [and] the companion of his manhood must react on their own condition to the degradation of his mental & moral being', she wrote.[150] She was 'firmly convinced that the division of mankind into two castes, one born to rule over the other, is . . . an unqualified mischief; a source of perversion and

---

[144] *Ibid.*, 48 (see also *CW* XXI, 390).   [145] *Ibid.*, 21.
[146] *Ibid.*, 41, 68–9 (see also *CW* XXI, 384).   [147] *Ibid.*, 22.   [148] *Ibid.*, 10–11.
[149] *Ibid.*, 98–108 (see also Taylor Mill and Mill, 'The Case of Mary Ann Parsons' 1 and 2 and 'The Case of Anne Bird', 1151–3, 1164–7, 1153–7).
[150] *Ibid.*, 12.

demoralisation, both to the favoured class and to those at whose expense they are favoured'.[151] It produced 'none of the good which it is the custom to ascribe to it, and form[ed] a bar ... to any really vital improvement, either in the character or in the social condition of the human race'.

One of her radical solutions was to propose co-education (unheard of at the time, though called for by some other feminists), because single-sex education 'induces a mystery in the feeling of the sexes towards each other', which is harmful in the long term.[152]

One reason it is harmful is because of the sexual double standard in society, by which men can try to penetrate this 'mystery', but girls are kept rigidly to a standard of 'purity'. Taylor Mill asserted that three-quarters of men in her contemporary society used the services of sex workers, and the lack of outrage over this in society was, she felt, to be lamented as it signalled that society was not going to readily change.[153] Her anger was not solely aimed at men; however – she felt that *all* women 'purchase[d]' things by sex – it might be 'a home, an establishment, a reputation' or just 'money', but it was a purchase nonetheless.

She also noted that men, as well as women, were 'caged' by society in the sense that 'eccentricity' in either sex was frowned upon, and visited by public obloquy. Again, though, there was a gender-based disparity and something of a double standard, 'society allowing to them [that is, to men] a cage large enough for short flights they do not wound their wings at every attempt to expand them as women do against their gilded bars'.[154]

Taylor Mill, then, identified both the patriarchy and many of the ways it harmed women (and men), not least through the social construction of their genders which prevented both from cultivating and developing their characters to the highest degree, and thus from achieving both the greatest happiness of which each was capable, and the greatest happiness of the greatest number. These were not unique insights among 'first-wave' feminists, but hers are nonetheless distinctive, and interesting in their emphasis on utilitarian ethics and the importance of 'the free development of individuality' for *everyone's* well-being as early as the 1830s.

'Perfect equality' between the sexes was her solution (including joint, and equal, education for both), and she had some hopes that the general trend of history, as well as a particular self-view by contemporary English society, meant that this would be achieved in the not-too-distant future. This said, given her view of women's oppression over thousands of years, she might not be surprised (though surely she would be disappointed) that almost 200 years after her

---

[151] *Ibid.*, 55.   [152] *Ibid.*, 13.   [153] *Ibid.*   [154] *Ibid.*, 152–3.

earliest writings, that 'tenth step' to true equality has not yet been taken, leaving us still little more than 'half-way' there.

5 Women's Rights

Only a handful of works now attributed to Harriet Taylor Mill were published in her lifetime.[155] The longest, and by far the most famous and influential, is *The*

---

[155] A review and a couple of poems were published in the 1830s. I will refer to *Enfranchisement* as being by Taylor Mill here, in line with general practice. It is worth noting, though, that there is some scholarly debate as to Mill's involvement. Certainly Mill was involved in some way in its production – not least, he seems (though presumably in discussion with Taylor Mill) to have decided on its title, rejecting that suggested by the editor of *The Westminster Review*, where *Enfranchisement* was published (Robson, 'Textual Introduction', lxxv). Mill himself described his role as that of 'little more than that of editor and amanuensis' – in line with this, Robson suggests that the final manuscript was probably in Mill's handwriting (Mill, CW XXI, 393; Robson, 'Textual Introduction', lxxv). The question of Mill's involvement really revolves around what he meant by 'little more'.

Mill noted that Taylor Mill's authorship was 'known at the time, and publicly attributed to her' (Mill, 'Introduction', 393). When reprinted after her death, *Enfranchisement* was ascribed to 'Mrs Stuart Mill' (Robson, 'Textual Introduction', lxxvii) (In this, though, the publisher may merely have been following Mill's lead – in suggesting the publication, Mill referred to 'Mrs Mill's paper' – Mill, Letter 1084, to Herbert Spencer, 24 May 1867, CW XVI, 1270). Mill himself was keen both to deny it was his own work and to credit Taylor Mill's authorship (Mill, Letter 61, to Anna Blackwell, 16 August 1851, CW XIV, 75; Mill, Letter 1314, to J. S. Bird, 3 November 1868, CW XVI, 1476; Mill, Letter 1294, to George Thatcher, 27 September 1868, CW XVI, 1451; Robson, 'Textual Introduction', lxxvi–lxxvii; Mill, Letter 825, to Edwin Chadwick, 28 May 1865, CW XVI, 1059; Mill, Letter 876, to Moncure Daniel Conway, 23 October 1865, CW XVI, 1106–7; Mill, Letter 1502, to Paulina Wright Davis, 11 December 1869, CW XVII, 1670). The only exception is when approaching the editor of the *Westminster* regarding publication where, as Miller points out, Mill said 'if you are inclined for an article on the Emancipation of Women ... I have one nearly ready' (Miller, 'Harriet Taylor'). This might suggest Mill authored *Enfranchisement*, or had a larger role in its composition, than he later admitted – it might, on the other hand, be ascribable to Mill contacting an editor (whom he knew) on Taylor Mill's part (the 'I' might be like that used by an agent or editor, not an author) and/or to Taylor Mill's dislike of publicity (perhaps she did not want to be known publicly as the author, particularly at this point in her life, where her recent widowhood and engagement to Mill to some extent highlighted the unconventionality of her earlier personal life). Relatedly, a contemporary gifted a copy of *Enfranchisement* by Taylor Mill's eldest son reported that Taylor Mill said Mill had written it, and 'he says she did' (Miller, 'Harriet Taylor'). It is not clear, however, that this is anything more than hearsay. If it *is*, it might reflect Taylor Mill's dislike of publicity in general, or, again, a diffidence about her name – and ideas – being in the public sphere connected to this topic. It could also reflect a generosity in her view of Mill's contribution, which should be balanced with his own view.

Concerning the idea that Mill's role was larger than he later acknowledged, when writing to Taylor Mill about a possible reprint, Mill noted that when *Enfranchisement* was published in a selection of 'his' essays (as it was, in 1859), it would be 'preceded by a preface which will show that much of all my later articles, and all the best of that one, were, as they were, my Darling's'. This might suggest a larger role than that of 'editor and amanuensis', which was how he described his involvement in the published introduction of the collection (Mill, Letter 146, to Taylor Mill, 20 March 1854, CW XIV, 189–90). On the other hand, we might think the published version more accurate than the letter. Similarly, Mill agreed they should not reprint of *Enfranchisement* because 'I should not like any more than you do that that paper should be supposed to be the best that we could do, or the real expression of our mind on the subject',

Enfranchisement of Women. This is partly a review of recent events regarding the campaign for women's suffrage in America, and partly a series of arguments for giving votes to British women. As well as championing women's right to vote, Taylor Mill advocated for their rights to equal educations and access to jobs and career opportunities with men.

Enfranchisement was published in *The Westminster Review* in 1851. Taylor Mill seems to have been working on an essay on this theme for a few years – certainly, in 1849, Mill urged her to finish 'your pamphlet – or little book, rather, for it should be that' on the subject of women.[156] Some manuscripts remain, in both Taylor Mill and Mill's handwriting, from around this period on the broad subject of women's rights.[157] These may have been part of the earlier 'pamphlet' mentioned or – as John Robson argued[158] – 'preparatory' for *Enfranchisement* (or both). Certainly, they have some connection to Mill's *Subjection of Women*, which was published in 1869, but first written in 1860, and which he described as drawing on a 'fund of thought' developed with Taylor Mill since the 1830s.[159]

Actually, Taylor Mill was not fond of the phrase 'women's rights'. This was because she felt that '[t]he rights of women are no other than the rights of human beings'.[160] However, she recognised that the phrase needed to be used because

---

which might also suggest Mill had a larger role in *Enfranchisement* (*ibid.*). On the other hand, this might only signal that Mill felt a reprint 'years after, under our own auspices as a pamphlet' would give it authority as *their* view, which 'a mere review article written on a special occasion' did not have. This does not necessarily mean he had a significant role in writing *Enfranchisement*, only that people might think he had had such a role if the work was re-published.

Overall, then, I agree with Robson that '[o]ne may safely conclude that the article is, on the common understanding of authorship … Taylor-Mill's' (Robson, 'Textual Introduction', lxxvii). That is, the arguments, both in terms of content and expression, are largely Taylor Mill's, though we should recognise Mill's role in editing it, and in encouraging Taylor Mill to write it (roles she also played in respect to Mill in their wider co-authoring relationship – Mill, *Autobiography*, 255–7). As Robson says, however, seeing Mill as a 'co-author' of *Enfranchisement* risks underplaying what we mean when we say Taylor Mill was the 'co-author' of some of his texts (most obviously, *On Liberty*), where what is meant is a much more significant role in composing content and determining how key ideas are framed and expressed. Mill and Taylor Mill were evidently very careful about the exact published form of *Enfranchisement* (Mill told the publisher that it was 'necessary on such a subject to be as far as possible invulnerable' – Robson, 'Textual Introduction', lxxv). And evidently, this was a topic close to Mill's heart on which he and Taylor Mill had shared ideas for around twenty years: it would be surprising, then, if Mill had significantly disagreed with the arguments of *Enfranchisement*, even if feeling it was not the 'full' expression of either Taylor Mill's or his own thoughts on this subject. But the book should be seen as primarily Taylor Mill's, and I treat it was such in this section.

[156] Mill, Letter 6, to Taylor Mill, 21 February 1849, *CW* XIV, 13.
[157] See Mill and Taylor Mill, 'Papers on Women's Rights', 378–92.   [158] *Ibid.*, 378.
[159] Mill, *Autobiography*, 265.   [160] Taylor Mill, *Complete Works*, 43.

'law and opinion, having been made chiefly by men, have refused to recognise in women the universal claims of humanity'. This said, she believed that

> When opinion on this subject shall be further advanced towards rectifications, neither 'rights of women' nor even 'equality of women' will be terms in use, because neither of them fully expresses the real object to be aimed at, viz, the negation of all distinctions among persons, grounded on the accidental circumstance of sex.

Her 'Principle' was 'perfect equality'.[161]

Taylor Mill thought that the social, economic and political 'disability' of women based on their sex was, in itself, 'an evil' and 'a grievance'.[162] She did not think women ought to have to point to something they positively lost by, for instance, not being able to vote – that they were excluded merely on the grounds of sex was a wrong in itself. People who asked women what *good* it would do them to become an elector were missing the point:

> What these people . . . think there is no harm in cutting off from the life of any body . . . is precisely what makes the chief value of life. They think you lose nothing as long as you are not prevented from having what you have and doing what you do: now the value of life does not consist in what you or do, but in what you may have or do. Freedom, power, and hope, are the charms of existence. If you are outwardly comfortable, they think it nothing to cut off hope, to close the region of possibilities, to say that you shall have no carrieré, no excitement, that neither chance nor your own exertions shall ever make your anything more or other than you now are.[163]

It was this scope for freedom (for doing 'as you please') which Taylor Mill thought women had a right to (a right which men currently enjoyed, even though it was curtailed by socio-economic position and the class-bound prejudices and institutions of contemporary society). This is worth bearing in mind when considering some of her more specific arguments – the right to vote, for instance, was necessary as a step towards achieving this wider liberty, rather than being the end goal of feminist campaigning.

Indeed, 'first-wave' feminists can sometimes be criticised for thinking that if only women were granted equal rights, they would achieve actual equality, and there would be no further need for feminism (or further feminist complaints to make about society). Taylor Mill certainly saw equal rights as of fundamental importance to women's freedom and equality (without them, women would always remain unequal), but she was also well aware that attitudes towards women and their 'proper role' in life needed to change. Some of this change would have to happen before the law would change, but this does not mean she

---

[161] *Ibid.*, 46.   [162] *Ibid.*, 37.   [163] *Ibid.*, 38.

did not see that a lot would need to change even when the law had changed. After all, what she wanted was to ensure for women the equal opportunity to 'freely develop their individuality' and to maximise their own happiness, consistent with equal happiness for all (and thereby contribute to the greatest happiness of the greatest number) – and these are wider goals than merely securing equal rights, though unachievable without securing them. Changing the law, and the attitudes which currently prevent legal change, however, was clearly a necessary first step.

When considering why women need the vote, we can see the wide range of rights Taylor Mill thought women needed (and areas where their rights needed improving). Before answering the question 'what is the use of giving women the vote', she said, we need to determine 'what is the use of votes at all?' because '[w]hatever use there is in any case, there is in the case of women':

> Are votes given to protect the particular interests of the voters? Then women need votes, for the state of the law as to their property, their rights with regard to children, their right to their own person, together with the extreme mal-administration of the courts of justice in cases of even the most atrocious violence when practiced by men to their wives,[164] contributes a mass of grievance greater than exists in the case of any other class or body of persons. Are votes given as a means of fostering the intelligence of the voters, and enlarging their feelings by directing them to a wider class of interest? This would be as beneficial to women as to men. Are votes given as a means of exalting voters in social position and estimation? and to avoid making, an offensive distinction to their disadvantage? This reason is strong in the case of women. And this reason would suffice in the absence of any other. Women should have votes because otherwise they are not the equals but the inferiors of men. So clear is this, that any one who maintains that it is right in itself to exclude women from votes, can only do it for the express purpose of stamping on them the character of inferiors.[165]

'The greatest good that can be done for women', she argued, 'is to recognise them as citizens – as substantive members of the community instead of mere things belonging to members of the community'.[166] At the very foundation of the subject of women's equality was 'the question . . . whether it is right and expedient that one-half of the human race should pass through life in a state of forced subordination to the other half'.[167] Taylor Mill's answer was a resounding 'no', and she pointed out that the *real* reason people ever said 'yes' 'is that men like it'.

Taylor Mill was strongly opposed to the idea that women had to be 'in a state of compulsory obedience to any other human being (except as the mere organ

---

[164] These are all themes in her co-authored articles with Mill in the decade preceding the writing of these notes (c.1850–1).
[165] Taylor Mill, *Complete Works*, 43, 48.   [166] *Ibid.*, 48.   [167] *Ibid.*, 62.

and minister of the law)', and the fact that women had to swear obedience to their husbands (and that husbands took that literally and seriously) was one of her many criticisms of marriage.[168] Fathers, too, generally expected obedience of their daughters, and few women were living neither in their father's house nor their husband's. Women needed the right to be independent, to live under their own will – to be, in the phrase found in *On Liberty,* 'sovereign' 'over their own body and mind'.[169] That they were not allowed to be autonomous 'will', she argued, 'be acknowledged to be as monstrous an infraction of the rights and dignity of humanity as slavery is at last', or – at least – so she hoped.[170] Indeed, she argued that '[t]he evils of women's present condition lie in the necessity of dependence'.[171]

Women also needed the right to enter into any occupations they chose (and the right to achieve the right sorts of entry requirements, where those were relevant, if they were capable of doing so): contemporary legal barriers to women entering certain professions (or doing certain qualifications, for instance, becoming a doctor) ought to be eradicated.[172] As she put it:

> Good laws, laws which pay any due regard to human liberty, will not class human beings according to mere general presumptions, nor require them to do one thing and to abstain from another on account of any supposed suitableness to their natural or acquired gifts, but will leave them to class themselves under the natural influence of those and of all the other peculiarities of their situation, which if left free they will not fail to do quite as well, not to say much better, than any inflexible law made for them by pedantic legislators or conceited soi-disant philosophers are ever likely to do.[173]

To ensure independence even with such 'good laws', women would also need to be able to own their own property, and have a right to their own earnings when married. They would also need the 'right' to their own person, as Taylor Mill puts it[174] – that is, marital rape ought to be recognised as rape (and as a crime), and women should no longer be forced, or expected, to have sex with their husbands whenever he demanded, or to be viewed by their husbands as continually sexually available to them, with their marriage vow representing never-

---

[168] *Ibid.,* 45.   [169] See Mill and Taylor-Mill, *On Liberty,* 224.
[170] Taylor Mill, *Complete Works,* 45.   [171] *Ibid.,* 47.   [172] *Ibid.,* 47, 50.
[173] *Ibid.,* 45–6. 'soi-disant' means 'so-called' or 'self-styled'. Given her anger over some elements of Mill's correspondence with Comte, particularly on the question of 'the division of the functions of men' which, as she rightly noted, would apply not just to different types of men, but to 'men & women', thus potentially barring women, by law, from certain positions in politics and the economy in Comte's ideal world (*Ibid.,* 31), she may have had Comte in mind here. But she might just as easily have had a whole range of philosophers, from Plato onwards, who have thought people's roles in life and society can be dictated by law rather than being left to their free choice.
[174] See, for example, *Ibid.,* 50.

ending consent to sexual intercourse. (This has been a long-running battle for feminists, with marital rape only recognised as a crime in Britain in 1991, well over a hundred years after Taylor Mill's death.)

Taylor Mill noted that, at present, many objections to women's equality (and to the 'good laws' just described) were 'based on the supposition that conceding equal political rights to women would be contrary to the interests of men', either their 'real' interests or their merely 'selfish' ones.[175] This she strongly objected to, believing instead that equality 'would be not only in accordance with, but greatly advantageous to the interests of men', as is only to be expected given her analysis of the way men, too, suffer because of the patriarchy (even though benefitting from it a great deal more than women). She recognised that a significant hurdle to get over when it came to women's equal political rights was the sense people had that it did not fit with their 'domestic servitude', which people were (generally) keen to see continued. She offered a variety of arguments both against women's 'proper sphere' being the home and against homemaking being a barrier to participating in politics.[176]

She was also very aware that many men campaigning for an extension to the suffrage (to working-class men) did not also think it should be extended to women, and this she thought hypocritical, revealing these so-called radicals real desire merely to tyrannise: 'The Chartist who denies the suffrage of women', she argued, 'is a Chartist only because he is not a lord: he is one of those levellers who would level down only to themselves'.[177] (Chartism was a mass movement, particularly in the 1840s, for – among other things – extending the franchise to working men and reforming Parliament.)

Moreover, 'custom' was against change – as it always was. 'Women never have had equal rights with men', and for some that was enough to explain why they never should have them.[178] This said, she felt it was 'the boast of modern Europeans, and of their American kindred, that they know and do many things which their forefathers neither knew nor did', and that it was 'perhaps the most unquestionable point of superiority in the present above former ages, that habit is not now the tyrant it formerly was over opinions and modes of action, and that the worship of custom is a declining idolatry'. Gender inequality, then, ought not to be persevered merely because it always had existed.

Taylor Mill also knew it was not just men who opposed women's equality. She noted that 'persons usually mean by virtues the qualities which are useful or convenient to themselves', and that women themselves believed the man-serving diktat that 'the paramount virtue of womanhood is loyalty to men'.[179] Men (which very much suits them) are seen as virtuous if they are 'self-will[ed]

---

[175] *Ibid.*, 47.   [176] *Ibid.*, 57–60.   [177] *Ibid.*, 54.   [178] *Ibid.*, 55.   [179] *Ibid.*, 63.

and self-asserti[ve]', whereas women (which, again, suits men) are encouraged to view 'abnegation of self, patience, resignation, and submission to power' as feminine virtues and 'graces' to which they ought to aspire. 'The meaning', she argued of these 'virtues', was 'merely, that power makes itself the centre of moral obligation, and that a man likes to have his own will, but does not like that his domestic companion should have a will different from his'. Some of women's opposition to their own equality, then, comes from a genuine and deep-rooted belief that they ought not to be equal, and that it would be immoral if they were, or if they were to exercise any of the 'masculine' virtues that equality would demand.

Similarly, Taylor Mill acknowledged that many women desired freedom and equality, but would not risk saying so in public, it being very much in their interest not to do so:

> Their position is like that of the tenant or labourers who vote against their own political interest to please their landlords of employers; with the unique addition, that submission is inculcated on them from childhood, as the peculiar attention and grace of their character. They are taught to think, that to repel actively even an admitted injustice done to themselves, is somewhat unfeminine, and had better be left to some male friend or protector. To be accused of rebelling against anything which admits of being called an ordinance of society, they are taught to regard as an imputation of a serious offence, to say the least, against the proprieties of their sex. It requires unusual moral courage as well as disinteredness in a woman, to express opinions favourable to women's enfranchisement, until, at least, there is some prospect of obtaining it.[180]

Moreover, many women who did engage publicly with the issue, but argued *against* equality, did so because that was also in their interest (whether or not they really believed it):

> The literary class of women, especially in England, are ostentatious in disclaiming the desire for equality or citizenship, and proclaiming their complete satisfaction with the place which society assigns to them; exercising in this ... a most noxious influence over the feelings and opinions of men, who unsuspectingly accept the servilities of toadyism as concessions to the force of truth, not considering that it is in the personal interest of these women to profess whatever opinions they expect will be agreeable to men.

Taylor Mill also asserted that some women's opposition to 'women's rights' stemmed from a fear that they would have to work – 'their lively imagination exaggerates the disagreeables of having to work instead of being worked for'

---

[180] *Ibid.*, 71.

and 'their education having precluded all notions of public spirit or personal dignity, far from being revolted at the idea of dependence' they see 'submission ... [as] a virtue'.[181] She felt such women 'enormously exaggerate both the talent and the labour required for the external details of life' and were 'unaware that they give as much labour and fritter away as much talent in executing badly' the domestic duties they insisted were a good argument against 'women's emancipation'. 'Is it not true', she asked, 'that half the time of half the women in existence is passed in worthless and trashy work, of no benefit to any human being'?[182] Women did *not* need to spend all day in domestic work for all necessary domestic work to be done – and domestic work itself (indeed, all work, in itself) was no barrier to political participation.

In Mill's *Autobiography* he said he and Taylor Mill 'looked forward to a time when society will no longer be divided into the idle and the industrious', and this applies as much to the 'division' between middle- and upper-class men and their wives as it does to the whole of the landowning and/or capital-owning class, and the working class.[183] Similarly, in *Principles of Political Economy*, Taylor Mill (and Mill) said:

> I do not recognise as either just or salutary, a state of society in which there is any 'class' which is not labouring; any human beings, exempt from bearing their share of the necessary labours of life, except those unable to labour, or who have fairly earned rest by previous toil.[184]

Again, the context is the traditional sense of 'class' (working, or 'middle'/'upper'), but it applies just as well to men and women, and we can therefore imagine that Taylor Mill had little truck with the desire not to work which she lays at the door of some women who oppose equality (though Taylor Mill herself never had any paid employment, or an education which would have necessarily fitted her for any of the professions even if she could have legally taken any of them up, particularly once married). She insisted that people who had once tasted independence would not agree to go back to being dependent, and it seems she thought that as much of women as of workers.[185]

Relatedly, Taylor Mill argued against those who said that women ought not to be made equal (especially in the economic sphere) as this 'would be an injurious addition to the crowd of competitors, by whom the avenues to almost all kinds of employment are choked up, and its remuneration depressed'.[186] Firstly, she dismissed this argument against women's suffrage because it was economic, not

---

[181] *Ibid.*, 47.   [182] *Ibid.*, 48.   [183] Mill, *Autobiography*, 239.

[184] Mill, *Principles of Political Economy*, 758.

[185] *Ibid.*, 761–2. See also Taylor Mill, *Complete Works*, 138.

[186] Taylor Mill, *Complete Works*, 60.

political – it could not be used to deny women citizenship. Secondly, even if the argument was true, Taylor Mill countered, and 'that to lay open to women the employments now monopolised by men, would tend, like the breaking down of other monopolies, to lower the rate of remuneration in those employments', what evil would ensue? 'The worst ever asserted, much worse than is likely at all to be realised, is that if women competed with men, a man and a woman could not together earn more than is now earned by the man alone.'

Suppose this was true, she continued, and 'the joint income of the two would be the same as before', what would have changed would be that 'the woman would be raised from the position of a servant to that of a partner'. This was 'infinitely preferable' to contemporary society, even if nothing else changed. Part of the income would be 'the woman's earning', and it was far better that this was so, even if the total income remained the same, than 'that she should be compelled to stand aside in order that men may be the sole earners, and the sole dispensers of what is earned'. Even under existing law, Taylor Mill felt, 'a woman who contributes materially to the support of the family, cannot be treated in the same contemptuously tyrannical manner as one who, however she may toil as a domestic drudge, is a dependent on the man for subsistence'.[187] Taylor Mill even thought that domestic violence might decrease if women contributed the household income, not least because women would be less dependent on men, and more able to leave a violent situation.[188]

Moreover, if wages *were* depressed, 'remedies will be found … in time', including potentially 'a more rigid exclusion of children from industrial employment'. (In the longer term, more socialist developments might do away with wage labour, and thus with competition for wages, and their depression through this competition or increased numbers of labourers in the market, altogether – a subject I will move onto in the next section.) She concluded:

> [S]o long as competition is the general law of human life, it is tyranny to shut out one half of the competitors. All who have attained the age of self-government have an equal claim to be permitted to sell whatever kind of useful labour they are capable of, for the price which it will bring.

(The contrast with the arguments in *Subjection* is interesting. There, Mill argued that married women, at least, should see domestic duties as having the first claim on their labour, unless they were supremely talented at some other job, at least when their children were small, and/or unless they can get someone else – presumably a woman, as Mill seemed to take it as read that, at least in contemporary non-ideal society, men would refuse to do domestic labour – to

---

[187] *Ibid.*, 60–1.   [188] *Ibid.*, 61.

perform these domestic labours for them.[189] This is more closely aligned with what Mill wrote in his *On Marriage* than anything we see in Taylor Mill's work, and may reflect solely his ideas.[190])

Taylor Mill, then, defended and argued for a wide range of rights for women. She saw them as 'the rights of human beings', rights which everyone needed in order to live a flourishing life, freely develop their individuality and maximise both their own and everyone else's happiness. The individual rights she defended are not, therefore, an exhaustive list of what might be needed to secure women's equality and freedom, but some important first steps in the right direction, such as rights to their own property, to their own person (from assault, particularly sexual assault), to their children, to work, to education and to vote. Many of her arguments were aimed at a middle-class audience (particularly men), because they were vote holders with the power to change things, but her arguments (particularly about work) have a wider application.

She was acutely aware of the impact of power differentials in relation-ships, and campaigned for legal rights for women which would at least mitigate these differences. She sought radical solutions, particularly in economic transformation. She wanted to free women from what she called 'domestic servitude' through ensuring only 'useful' domestic work was done and ensuring that women were educated and legally able to take advantage of other employment opportunities. This said, she never overtly argued, or called for (as more modern feminists have done) men to take their fair share of domestic labour, though this might be implicit in her arguments that there is no particular labour for which either men or women are naturally 'fit', and that everyone should 'bear[...] their share of the neces-sary labours of life', domestic labour (such as cooking) being highly 'neces-sary' for everyone to survive.

Taylor Mill's advocacy of women's rights from a unique perspective of a utilitarianism which sees the individual's 'free development of individu-ality' as central to utility, and wants to maximise the happiness of all consistent with the greatest happiness of each, should secure her place at least in the canon of the history of feminist thought. Her arguments and the goal of her campaigns may have been overtaken by history and develop-ments in feminist theory, but her central emphasis on women's equal right to equality, liberty and happiness remains powerful and worth re-affirming even in modern times.

---

[189] See Mill, *Subjection of Women*, 297–8 and McCabe, 'Good Housekeeping?', 135–55.

[190] This difference is also often flagged to 'prove' that *Enfranchisement* is solely Taylor Mill's work, and that she was more radical in her feminism than Mill.

6 Socialism

Harriet Taylor Mill's family were relatively conservative, but she was a radical by the time she was in her late teens, and mixed in radical circles with her new, and similarly radical, husband. However, although she would have described herself as a 'Democrat' in the 1830s, by the mid-to-late 1840s, she and John Stuart Mill thought of themselves as 'under the general designation of Socialists'.[191]

Taylor Mill's 'Democratic' commitments included '[n]o hereditary privileges whatsoever', '[n]o exclusion from the suffrage', '[c]omplete freedom of speech, printing, public meetings and associations, locomotion, and industry in all its branches', '[n]o church establishments of paid clergy; but national schools and colleges without religion', '[a]ll occupations alike to be open to men and women; and all kinds and departments of instruction', '[t]he property of intestates[192] to belong to the state, which then undertakes the education, and setting out in life, of all descendants not otherwise provided for' and '[n]o one to acquire by gift or benefit more than a limited amount'.[193] Although much of this chimes with the campaigns of other radicals at the time, it is still worth emphasising how radical this agenda was in terms of both destroying old institutions (such as the landed aristocracy) and ensuring equality. Indeed, this 'democratic' vision is radically more equal and free than contemporary UK society, with an unelected House of Lords, significant inequalities exacerbated by private education and the passing of immense fortunes between generations, and an established church.

Taylor Mill and Mill recorded that, during the 1840s, they felt that because education was 'so wretchedly imperfect', they 'dreaded the ignorance and especially the selfishness and brutality of the mass' – that is, they were concerned about the actions of a government elected by universal suffrage, and therefore representing the interests of the working-class majority.[194] They thought that contemporary events (for instance, violence associated with Chartism) did not bode well for a more democratic future (though retaining their commitment to universal suffrage) – a tyranny of the majority was better than a tyranny of the minority, but no tyranny at all was best.

Taylor Mill's concern about poor education and its political effects, however, did not make her support what she and Mill called 'patriarchal' institutions – where the rich ought to be '*in loco parentis*' to the poor.[195] For one thing, this was 'imaginative' rather than realistic, 'an idealisation':

---

[191] Mill, *Autobiography*, 239.   [192] That is, people who die without making a will.
[193] Taylor Mill, *Complete Works*, 50.   [194] Mill, *Autobiography*, 239.
[195] Mill, *Principles of Political Economy*, 759. Mill accords Taylor Mill a significant role in writing, in particular, the chapter 'On the Probable Futurity of the Labouring Classes', which I quote from here. The chapter, he said, 'was entirely due to her', and she was responsible for the thrust of the chapter's argument (that there are two options for the future of the working classes – dependence

All privileged and powerful classes, as such, as have used their power in the
interest of their own selfishness, and have indulged their self-importance in
despising ... those who were, in their estimation, degraded, by the being
under the necessity of working for their benefit.[196]

For another, working people simply would not put up with it: 'Of the working
men, at least in the more advanced countries of Europe, it may be pronounced
certain, that the patriarchal or paternal system of government is one to which
they will not again be subject.'[197] Workers could read, could access newspapers
and political tracts (including those written by members of their own class), and
were preached to by dissenting, often radical, ministers who called on them to
use their own faculties, not just blindly believe 'the creeds professed ... by their
superiors'. They had been brought together in factories by the demands of
industrialisation and the division of labour; railways allowed them to travel,
and change employers 'as easily as their coats'; and they had been 'encouraged
to seek a share in the government, by means of the electoral franchise'.[198] All of
this meant that '[t]he working classes have taken their interests into their own
hands, and are perpetually showing that they think the interests of their employers not identical with their own, but opposite to them'. Thus, 'to their own
qualities must now be commended the care of their destiny'.[199]

Taylor Mill and Mill felt '[t]here is no reason to believe that prospect other
than hopeful', particularly (though not solely) because of socialist develop-
ments led by workers to transform the economy and with it society more
generally. As Mill put it, recalling their joint position:

> While we repudiated with the greatest energy that tyranny of society over the
> individual which most Socialistic systems are supposed to involve, we yet
> looked forward to a time when society will no longer be divided into the idle
> and the industrious; when the rule that they who do not work shall not at, will
> be applied not to paupers only, but impartially to all; when the division of the
> produce of labour, instead of depending, as in so great a degree it does now,
> on the accident of birth, will be made by concert, on an acknowledged
> principle of justice; and when it will no longer either be, or be thought to
> be, impossible for human beings to exert themselves strenuously in procuring
> benefits which are not to be exclusively their own, but to be shared with the
> society they belong to. The social problem of the future we considered to be,
> how to unite the greatest individual liberty of action, with a common owner-
> ship in the raw material of the globe, and an equal participation of all in the

---

or independence), this being 'wholly an exposition of her thoughts, often in words taken from her
own lips'. As Taylor Mill died before the sixth (1862) edition, I am only quoting passages from
those chapters of the first five editions in which, according to Mill at least, she had both initial
authorial, and editorial, input. See Mill, *Autobiography*, 255–7.
[196] Mill, *Principles of Political Economy*, 760.   [197] *Ibid.*, 761–2.   [198] *Ibid.*, 762.
[199] *Ibid.*, 763.

benefits of combined labour. We had not the presumption to suppose that we could already foresee, by what precise form of institutions these objects could most effectually be attained, or at how near or how distant a period they would become practicable. We saw clearly that to render any such social transformation either possible or desirable, an equivalent change of character must take place both in the uncultivated herd who now compose the labouring masses, and in the immense majority of their employers . . . [W]e regarded all existing institutions and social arrangements as being . . . 'merely provisional', and we welcome with the greatest pleasure and interest all socialistic experiments by select individuals (such as the Cooperative Societies), which, whether they succeeded or failed, could not but operate as a most useful education of those who took part in them, by cultivating their capacity of acting upon motives pointing directly to the general good.[200]

Socialism, to the modern reader, tends to mean Marxism, but Taylor Mill almost certainly knew nothing of Karl Marx or his ideas. Although she was alive when *The Communist Manifesto* was published (and she could have read it in the original German), it is unlikely she would have come across a copy. (The first English translation was published in 1850 in the Chartist magazine *The Red Republican*: this is never mentioned as something Taylor Mill had read, and it seems relatively unlikely that she would have done, particularly given her move away from 'democracy' and Chartism.) The first volume of Marx's most famous book *Capital* was not published until sixteen years after her death. Indeed, Marx himself only really became a prominent socialist almost twenty years after her death.

Instead of Marxism, what Taylor Mill knew of, and meant by, socialism, were the works of Henri Saint-Simon and his followers the Saint-Simonians; the writings of Etienne Cabet; the works of Charles Fourier mainly as transmitted by Victor Considerant; the ideas of Louis Blanc (who became a good friend of Mill's in the period of his exile in London, which coincided with Mill and Taylor Mill's early married life); and the works of Robert Owen, William Thompson and other 'co-operators', including many working-class people making their own cooperative experiments (for instance, the Rochdale Pioneers), and those writing and theorising about, and encouraging others to emulate, these endeavours, for instance George Jacob Holyoake, Philippe Buchez and Henri-Robert Feugeuray.[201]

Some of these thinkers are those dismissed by Marx and Engels as 'utopian' socialists, and it is true that many wrote detailed descriptions of ideal future societies (some of them, for instance, Cabet, even in fictionalised form). But

---

[200] Mill, *Autobiography*, 239–41.

[201] For more on what socialism meant to Mill (and Taylor Mill), see McCabe, *John Stuart Mill, Socialist*, 93–136.

many did not – not least Considerant, many of the Saint-Simonians, Thompson, Holyoake, Buchez and Feugeuray – and Mill recalled that he and Taylor Mill overtly eschewed as 'presumption' this detailed world-making for future societies. Instead, she and Mill pointed both to normative reasons why socialism was an improvement on capitalism, and to empirical data they thought suggested society was moving (perhaps inexorably) in a more socialist direction.

From her concerns about 'democracy', Taylor Mill can come across as opposed to the working class, perhaps as being rather snobbish. It is true that she (and Mill) had a low opinion of many individual workers, who – for instance – were motivated only by self-interest, and/or tried to do as little as possible at work. Similarly, she thought domestic violence was more common in the working classes (though by no means confined to them) and had a very low opinion of *any* men who were violent towards their wives. But though she had concerns about what might happen if the current working class were handed political power which could not be ameliorated or opposed, her hopes for the future were with a better-educated working population (which had to include women as well as men). She and Mill praised, for instance, 'the heroism and . . . public spirit and good sense of the working people of Paris' who had attempted the 'arduous task' of forming National Workshops and other kinds of producer and consumer cooperatives after the revolution of 1848,[202] and the 'capacity of exertion and self-denial in the masses of mankind, which', they added, 'is never known but on the rare occasions on which it is appealed to by the nature of some great idea of elevated sentiment', as it had been in the French Revolution of 1848.[203] She and Mill wrote of this time:

> For the first time, it then seemed to the intelligent and generous of the working classes of a great nation, that they had obtained a government who sincerely desired the freedom and dignity of the man, and who did not look upon it as their natural and legitimate state to be instruments of production, working for the benefit of the possessors of capital. Under this encouragement, the ideas sown by Socialist writers, of an emancipation of labour to be effected by means of association, throve and fructified; and many working people came to the resolution, not only that they would work for one another . . . but that they would also free themselves, at whatever cost of labour or privation, from the necessity of paying, out of the produce of their industry, a heavy tribute for the use of capital; that they would extinguish this tax, not by robbing the capitalists of what they or their predecessors had acquired by labour and preserved by economy, but by honestly acquiring capital for themselves.[204]

Her fear, then, was of a working-class majority who *would* 'rob . . . the capitalists' of their current wealth, not of a working class who would liberate

---

[202] Mill, *Principles of Political Economy*, 776.   [203] *Ibid.*, 775, 784.   [204] *Ibid.*, 775–6.

themselves from needing to make use of this wealth in order to work and flourish. Taylor Mill and Mill, as utilitarians, put great store by security – it was a matter of expediency as well as justice to compensate capitalists for their capital. Her admiration, though, (like Mill) is clear for workers who voluntarily underwent even great privation in order to 'honestly' free themselves of reliance on capitalists – that is, workers, as she and Mill describe it, who accrued their own capital from 'small sums which could be collected from their savings, or which were lent to them by other workpeople as poor as themselves', including those 'who have had nothing to rely on but their own slender means and the small loans of fellow-workmen, and who lived on bread and water while they devoted the whole surprise of their gains to the formation of a capital' sufficient to start a producer cooperative.[205]

Indeed, it was in the cooperative movement (and particularly producer cooperatives) that Taylor Mill and Mill put their hopes for both the future and the mode in which it might be achieved. These were '[t]he form of association ... which if mankind continue to improve, must be expected in the end to predominate'.[206]

> They have existed long enough to furnish the type of future improvement: they have exemplified the process for bringing about a change in society, which would combine the freedom and independence of the individual, with the moral, intellectual, and economical advantages of the democratic spirit, by putting an end to the division of society into the industrious and the idle, and effacing all social distinctions but those fairly earned by personal services and exertions. Associations ... by the very process of their success, are a course of education in those moral and active qualities by which alone success can be either deserved or attained.[207]

She and Mill envisaged a peaceful transition through cooperation, with more and more workers joining cooperatives, and capitalists finding it most profitable to invest in cooperatives rather than continue 'the struggle of the old system' of wage labour with 'workpeople of only the worst description' – that is, those with too little self-discipline and drive to join a cooperative. Eventually, they argued, capitalists might 'perhaps ... exchange their capital for terminable annuities'. Thus, '[i]n this or some such mode, the existing accumulations of capital might honestly, and by a kind of spontaneous process, become ... the joint property of all who participate in their employment'. This would be, they said:

> a transformation which ... (assuming of course that both sexes participate equally in the rights and in the government of the association) would be the

---

[205] *Ibid.*, 776. [206] *Ibid.*, 775. [207] *Ibid.*, 793.

nearest approach to social justice, and the most beneficial ordering of industrial affairs for the universal good, which it is possible at present to foresee.[208]

Taylor Mill was certain that working people would no longer agree to the
relationship 'between a capitalist as chief, and workpeople without a voice in
the management'.[209] Instead, workers would insist on 'the association of the
labourers themselves on terms of equality, collectively owning the capital with
which they carry on their operations, and working under managers elected and
removeable by themselves'.

Taylor Mill and Mill's socialist vision, therefore, was one where everyone
worked in a producer cooperative, and did their shopping in a consumer
cooperative. This would eradicate competition in the labour market, though
producer cooperatives might compete against each other in a market, albeit one
with a different incentive structure to contemporary capitalism.[210]

There were evidently normative gains to be made from socialism – workers
were independent (and more free); everyone would work (a significant
improvement for equality and justice); women's equality would be improved;
there would be all the improvements of a more 'democratic spirit' being more
widespread; and hierarchical social distinctions based on arbitrary bases such as
birth, blood, sex or inherited wealth would be eradicated. So, Taylor Mill had
a moral argument for socialism – it was a better way of organising society than
contemporary capitalism (and than the 'democratic' reforms she had previously
championed). In addition, she saw empirical data, such as workers' increased
demands for independence, and the success of the contemporary cooperative
movement, as pointing to the likelihood of a more socialist future.

The empirical side of her argument has failed the test of history – although
there are a number of extremely successful cooperatives around the world, we
do not all work in producer cooperatives, sourcing our consumer goods in
consumer cooperatives. (Even if we shop at the Coop in Britain, the people
serving us work for wages, which goes against the cooperative principle.) But
her moral arguments for socialism are still worth examining – to what extent are
we free and independent at work, and are there normative reasons for thinking it
would be better if we were freer or more autonomous? Why are there power
differentials between employers and employed, and are these always justified?
Why do we organise production in such a way as to include a competitive
market for labour, and aim only at the 'narrow' goal of increasing profits for
owners? Do women equally share in the power and government of the

---

[208] *Ibid.*, 793–4.   [209] *Ibid.*, 775.
[210] For more on this, see McCabe, 'John Stuart Mill and Fourierism', 35–61 and 'John Stuart Mill,
Market Socialist?', 506–27.

organisations in which they work, and if not, why not? In this, Taylor Mill offers a challenge to contemporary society which repays much thought.

Almost everything I have quoted in this section so far was co-authored with Mill. From Mill's description of their collaborative process, I think we are justified in thinking these quotes adequately represent Taylor Mill's views, as well as Mill's. This latter idea has, however, been challenged by some Mill scholars, who see Taylor Mill as 'more' socialist than Mill and, even, as persuading (or otherwise forcing) Mill to adopt 'more' socialist positions than he really believed.[211] (Thus, what I have quoted from their jointly authored works would represent Taylor Mill's views, but not Mill's.)

As I have argued elsewhere, however, I do not think this reading is warranted.[212] There is very little in Taylor Mill's single-authored work which refers to socialism, so the accusation is based on some very slim evidence from correspondence with Mill (of which we only have his side); some comments Mill makes in the *Autobiography*; and the fact that, probably after her death, Mill started to write a separate work on socialism (which both had decided they ought to do), of which all that was published, as *Chapters on Socialism*, is a critical engagement with the ideas of some contemporary socialists.

The critical elements of *Chapters* are very similar to critiques made in *Principles* (in sections co-authored with Taylor Mill). *Chapters* lacks the more positive elements found in *Principles*, but is also incomplete. It cannot really be seen, therefore, as a sign of Mill turning away from socialism after Taylor Mill's death. I also think the evidence from the correspondence is very slight, and without Taylor Mill's own side hard to base anything on apart from that Mill seems to have misunderstood some of her editorial comments, and postponed changing *Principles* until they could discuss edits in person.[213]

It has also been argued that Mill somewhat blindly followed Taylor Mill when it came, in particular, to an assessment of communism, and that, therefore, the views in *Principles* are hers, and not his. It is true that, when discussing the second edition of *Principles*, Mill and Taylor Mill evidently thought there should be relatively significant rewrites of the chapter of property where varieties of socialism (including communism) are discussed. Mill said that the thought in the first edition, that '[t]hose who have never known freedom from anxiety as to the means of subsistence are apt to overate what is gained for positive enjoyment by the mere absence of that uncertainty', which meant that the increase in utility gained through communism's securing of subsistence was overrated by socialists, was 'inserted' on Taylor Mill's 'proposition, & very

---

[211] Winch, *Wealth and Life*, 137; Stafford, 'How Can a Paradigmatic Liberal Call Himself a Socialist?', 327.
[212] See McCabe, *John Stuart Mill, Socialist*, 249–55.   [213] *Ibid.*

nearly in [her] ... words'.[214] However, when it came to the second edition, she apparently 'object[ed] ... strongly and totally' to this, which Mill felt was 'the strongest part of the argument ... against Communism'. He was keen to 'make up his mind' and also be sure she had changed hers, but added, 'by thinking sufficiently I should probably come to think the same – as is almost always the case, I believe *always* when we come to think long enough'.

Later, he also said that he 'saw on consideration that the objection to Communism on the ground of its making life a kind of dead level might admit of being weakened (though I think it never could be taken away) consistently with the principle of Communism, though the Communistic plans now before the public could not do it'.[215] He wondered whether she agreed with him that there were *more* objections to communism than those he had recently included against Fourierism (which was a form of socialism to which he and, through him, Taylor Mill had only recently been exposed), and that 'the objections now stated to Communism are valid', adding, 'if *you* do not think so, I certainly will not print [them] ... even if there were no other reason than the certainty I feel that I should never long continue of an opinion different from yours on a subject which you have fully considered'.

It is worth noting that, in the second edition of *Principles*, there *are* more criticisms raised of communism than of Fourierism, and that, although it is admitted that 'on the Communistic scheme ... there would be an end to all anxiety concerning the means of subsistence; and this would be much gained for human happiness', a number of other concerns are raised, most importantly, a lack of freedom.[216] Moreover, it is asserted that 'it is perfectly possible' to end anxiety over the means of subsistence 'in a society grounded on private property', a system which is also 'compatible with a far greater degree of personal liberty'. Mill and Taylor Mill wrote: 'The perfection of social arrangements would be to secure to all persons complete independence and freedom of action, subject to no restriction but that of not doing injury to others', which is not possible to achieve under communism. Discussion with Taylor Mill, then, may have changed Mill's mind on these questions, but the published version of *Principles* does not simply look like a slavish adherence to her ideas. Moreover, even if Taylor Mill felt some critiques of communism had less weight in 1849 than she had in 1848, the passage we find in the second edition, with its echoes of the harm principle and other elements of *On Liberty,* is very much in keeping with her political philosophy, not least her emphasis on

---

[214] Mill, *Principles of Political Economy*, 978; Mill, Letter 15, to Taylor Mill, 19 February 1849, *CW* III, 1027.

[215] Mill, Letter 16, 21 February 1849, *CW* III, 1028.

[216] Mill, *Principles of Political Economy*, 978.

'independence', and acting freely unless we cause unhappiness (or 'injury') to others. Mill's willingness to capitulate to Taylor Mill's opinion whenever they disagreed is, then, I think, prone to be exaggerated, and these particular discussions are not good evidence that Taylor Mill was necessarily 'more' left wing than Mill, or managed to make him 'more' left wing than he really was.

It is true that in the *Autobiography*, Mill says he was Taylor Mill's 'pupil' when it came to 'the application of philosophy to the exigencies of human society and progress', which would include the discussions about socialist schemes, and that she taught him 'boldness of speculation and cautiousness of practical judgement'.[217] She was, he said, 'much more courageous and far-sighted than without her I should have been, in anticipations of an order of things to come'. Thus:

> Those parts of my writings and especially of the *Political Economy* which contemplate possibilities in the future such as, when affirmed by Socialists, have been in general fiercely denied by political economists, would, but for her, either have been absent, or the suggestions would have been made much more timidly and in a more qualified form.

This said, she also 'repressed in me all tendencies that were really visionary', always being concerned with 'practical obstacles' to reform (or adopting any particular socialist scheme).

This might suggest that they had different ideas about the practicality of socialism – though it suggests, too, that sometimes Mill thought it was more practical than Taylor Mill did. It may also suggest a difference in opinion as to what ought to go into *Principles* – and Mill notes, for instance, that it was at Taylor Mill's suggestion that he included the chapter 'on the probable futurity of the labouring population', where cooperation is discussed at length (after 1852, and profit-sharing schemes before that, alongside the general discussion of whether the poor should be dependent or independent).

It may also reflect a different view as to what was pertinent for a book on political economy, and how radical *Principles* ought to be in what ideas for reform it considered. In the Preface to the second edition of *Principles* (1849), Mill and Taylor Mill wrote that 'the increased importance which the Socialist controversy has assumed since this work was written', that is, the events of 1848 in France, among others, 'has made it desirable to enlarge the chapter which treats of it; the more so, as the objections therein stated to the specific schemes propounded by some Socialists, have been erroneously understood as a general condemnation of all that is commonly included under that name'.[218] A separate

---

[217] Mill, *Autobiography*, 257.　　[218] Mill, *Principles of Political Economy*, xciv.

work is suggested (as in their letters, and their list of potential future topics), but this did not emerge in either's lifetime.

Similarly, in the Preface to the third edition (1852), Mill and Taylor Mill wrote that they were:

> far from intending that the statement ... of the objections to the best known Socialist schemes, should be understood as a condemnation of Socialism, regarded as the ultimate result of human progress. The only objection to which any great importance will be ... attached ... is the unprepared state of mankind in general, and of the labouring classes in particular; their extreme unfitness at present for any order of things, which would make any considerable demand on either their intellect or their virtue ... [T]he great end of social improvement should be to fit mankind by cultivation, for a state of society combining the greatest personal freedom with that just distribution of the fruits of labour, which the present laws of property do not profess to aim at. Whether, when this state of mental and moral cultivation shall be attained, individual property in some form (though a form very remote from the present) or community of ownership in the instruments of production and a regulated division of the produce, will afford the circumstances most favourable to happiness, and best calculated to bring human nature to its greatest perfection, is a question which must be left, as it safely may, to the people of that time to decide. Those of the present are not competent to decide it.
>
> The chapter on the 'Futurity of the Labouring Classes' has been enriched with the results of the experience afforded since this work was first published, by the cooperative associations in France. That important experience shows that the time is ripe for a larger and more rapid extension of association among labourers, than could have been successfully attempted before.[219]

Although this Preface was taken out of later editions, the content it refers to was retained in all editions (even after Taylor Mill's death), and overall it stands as a good summary of Taylor Mill and Mill's beliefs regarding socialism and its feasibility. Specific socialist schemes had their good points, but also their bad, and it was best left to the people of a future date to decide if we ought to adopt any one of them entirely. In the meantime, reform to the system of individual property was possible, and desirable, particularly through profit-sharing and cooperation. Moreover, cooperation, in itself, provided a mode of transforming the system of individual property into a system of collective property, but in an entirely voluntary and peaceful way, respecting the property rights of existing property owners while still liberating workers and leading to much greater equality.

One might read Mill in these Prefaces as professing an attitude towards socialism, and particularly cooperation, which he did not really believe, but

---

[219] *Ibid.*, xcv.

the simpler explanation would be that *Principles* represents his and Taylor Mill's carefully considered opinion, one which changed with the times and with increased empirical knowledge about socialism (and theoretical knowledge from reading a wider range of socialist theorists).

Taylor Mill's commitment to liberty and independence, then, as well as her commitment to 'perfect equality', applied to the economic sphere as well as the sociopolitical. She wanted to see workers (both men and women) 'independent' of capital, and working in ways which were self-directed and autonomous. She also wanted to see that transformation take place in a peaceful, voluntary way. The outcome would be a much freer, and much more equal society (though she did not endorse communism's goal of equal shares, seeing some benefit in 'fairly earned' social, and economic, distinctions). Again, in highlighting the possibilities of a decentralised, non-coercive, small-scale socialism, Taylor Mill offers much food for thought to contemporary audiences, as well as challenging us as regards the normative bases, and outcomes, of our own society (even without thinking socialism would be preferable, or feasible even if preferable). If we really are committed to liberty, shouldn't we be committed to freedom and independence in our working lives as well as our political and social activity? And if gendered power relations based on arbitrary bases such as sex are wrong, aren't at least some power relations in the world of work based on class?

7 Morality and Religion

Harriet Taylor Mill was a utilitarian, that is, broadly speaking, a subscriber to Bentham's 'Greatest Happiness Principle'. Although brought up in a conventionally religious household, by the time she married her first husband she was part of the radical 'free-thinking', Unitarian congregation in South Place Chapel, Finsbury. In 1834, the chapel's minister, Fox, left the Unitarian church and became a preacher of 'rationalism'. This seems to be a religious move which Taylor Mill also made, although still invoking God in letters, and possibly retaining a belief in a God who was omni-benevolent, but not omnipotent.[220]

Taylor Mill was evidently thinking seriously about ethical questions, faith and religion in the 1830s, around the time she met John Stuart Mill (who records that he was, perhaps uniquely in his generation, brought up an atheist[221]), and the 'utility of religion', as well as other ethical questions, remained important throughout their lives. Utilitarianism is the foundation of a range of her arguments, from freedom to women's equality, and from a very early stage she

---

[220] See, for example, Taylor Mill, *Complete Works*, 332, 366, 374, 392.
[221] Mill, *Autobiography*, 41–3.

equated the development of individuality with the maximisation of happiness.[222]

Bentham's maxim is usually written as 'the greatest happiness of the greatest number', and utilitarians thought of as people who think that securing the greatest happiness of the greatest number is the primary ethical goal. Thus, actions which tend to produce happiness (understood as pleasure and the absence of pain) are viewed as good, or right, while actions which tend to produce unhappiness (pain, or the absence of pleasure) are considered bad or wrong.[223] Taylor Mill parses Bentham's maxim as 'the greatest [happiness] of the greatest no., the greatest happiness of each consistent with the happiness of others', which is an interesting addition, though it is not clear (as she did not expand on this idea) exactly what this implies.[224] This said, fleshing out this idea might help meet one criticism often levelled at utilitarianism: that its adherents must support the random killing and organ harvesting of healthy people to save the lives of others in need of organ transplants.[225] However, if the greatest happiness of the greatest number has to be consistent with the greatest happiness of others, killing to save other lives is prohibited as this cannot be consistent with the happiness of the person (non-voluntarily) killed. Similarly, it might help against the charge that utilitarians must give all resources to 'utility monsters', who generate more utility per unit of resource than others.[226] We need not be sacrificed in the 'maw' of these monsters if everyone's greatest happiness has to be consistent with the greatest happiness of others.

This is not a way of parsing utilitarianism which Mill made use of in his famous essay *Utilitarianism*, published two years after Taylor Mill's death, but it seems to be the way she thought about trying to act ethically in her own life. The compromise she reached with her husband, and Mill, in the 1830s (and into the 1840s) assured the greatest happiness of the greatest number, consistent with the happiness of others (even if each person's happiness might individually have been greater, but others' much less, in a different set of circumstances).

Mill, when Taylor Mill first met him, was famous as a champion of utilitarianism as a political philosophy as well as a moral theory. It seems likely Taylor Mill had also read Bentham, and in some of her earliest writing she challenges the received wisdom, by Bentham's supporters as well as detractors, 'that all our notions are guided by self-interest' understood as 'selfishness'.[227] Taylor Mill thought that the very essence of utilitarianism was anti-selfish – it is, after all, an

---

[222] Taylor Mill, *Complete Works*, 13.   [223] For more on this, see Mill, *Utilitarianism*, 203–59.
[224] Taylor Mill, *Complete Works*, 13.
[225] For more on this, see MacAskill, Meissner and Chappell, 'The Rights Objection'.
[226] See Nozick, *Anarchy, State, and Utopia*, 41.   [227] Taylor Mill, *Complete Works*, 152.

ethical theory which asks us to consider the interests of others and act for the greatest happiness *of the greatest number* (not just our own greatest happiness). We could, she believed, have a strong sense of our own interests, and wish to pursue them, without doing this in a selfish manner, or being motivated by selfishness.

This said, she pushed back against people who preached self-lessness. '[O]n what possible ground', she asked, 'but that of the most sentimental absurdity are we to be interested for everyone *except* ourselves?' On Bentham's rule, every-one counts for one, and that includes ourselves. Indeed, throughout her life Taylor Mill asserted the rights of the self (and self-assertion), as well as the rights of others against encroachment or overreach on the part of some people, either individually or collectively. She insisted that 'each living being's real object must be his own happiness' and that 'in this desire he must be honest. . . . It is a condition of sentient existence'.[228] That is, people cannot lie about what makes them happy – even if they are self-deluding, they will find themselves acting in such a way as to achieve it. 'Everything but enjoyment is a means to the attainment of that end' – that is, of enjoyment, or happiness, itself.

Although opposed to selfishness, Taylor Mill was also vehemently opposed to what she called 'sentimentality', particularly about the virtue of self-sacrifice. 'Sentimental morality', as she put it, only makes two kinds of character: 'good intentioned but hopelessly weak people' (such, she said, as society has success-fully tried to make most women), and 'thorough hypocrites or silent egoists' ('generally to be found among men') – that is, people who *say* they are self-sacrificing, but who, when it comes to the test, do not suit actions to words.[229] She felt that '[s]entimentality' filled the place of 'poetry or religion' in many characters, giving to both religion and poetry an important role in the character development of 'every person who is not a mere dry stick or machine'.[230]

This said, she was more for poetry than for religion. She counted it as one of the 'popular fallacies' that 'what is useful & beautiful in the religious feeling is necessarily connected with any traditions on the subject – either Jewish, Christian, or any other'.[231] 'Religion', she said, 'is a name for what are recog-nised as high qualities of the head and heart. Poetry & integrity'. These, she felt, 'are to be found in perfection' in people who had given up religion 'on examination'. The most admirable people – those of 'the highest moral principles . . . rigidest integrity & most ardent admiration of the beauties of nature & keenest curiosity & deepest interest in the unknown powers & mysteries of the universe' – 'always have been to my knowledge entire disbelievers'.[232] She denied that 'the Bible is Holy', saying instead that '[i]t is

---

[228] *Ibid.*, 154. [229] *Ibid.*, 152–3. [230] *Ibid.*, 153. [231] *Ibid.*, 225. [232] *Ibid.*, 225–6.

in the highest degree immoral & indecent, cruel & unjust'. She also denied that 'Christianity is a Philosophy', saying it was instead the 'inculcation of a single virtue – Benevolence'.[233]

Taylor Mill recognised a religious function of 'consolation to the victims of society' (particularly in Catholic countries, explaining by this the survival of the Catholic Church).[234] 'How much I long', she wrote, 'to see noble buildings consecrated to nobler purposes than the repetition of old fables, whose old poetry does not make amends for the old coarseness ... & mischievous moralities'. Though Catholicism, and Christianity more broadly, had been useful at earlier points of history, and 'done immensely much for the world', she felt 'it must give way to ideas at once more practical & more elevated'. The answer was not Protestantism, but something which would cultivate 'spiritual ideas' in such a way as endorse and achieve '[e]quality as a principle and feeling' through appealing to both 'the understanding' (as Protestantism did) and 'the sensual' (as Catholicism did).

Perhaps a little bluntly, we can see Taylor Mill as referring to the way in which Protestantism – and particularly the dissenting Protestantism with which she was familiar – insisted that people, for instance, read the Bible for themselves, and exercised their intellectual faculties in worshipping God. Protestant services were held in the vernacular language, and many dissenting Protestants emphasised simplicity, even asceticism, in regards to places of worship and personal dress in order not to distract people's mind's from God and from serious intellectual engagement with questions of theology and morality. In contrast, Catholicism (at the time) still held services in Latin, and was, for Taylor Mill at least (visiting Catholic churches as a tourist), more linked with beautiful architecture; wonderful, inspiring music; great art; and other elements which appealed to, and intoxicated, the senses such as candles and incense. She evidently felt that both were important for a 'better' religion to inspire belief and motivate action – inspiration comes from beauty (and its appeal to the senses) as well as from good arguments. That is, a 'Religion de L'Avenir' (or the religion of the future) would need to appeal to both our 'understanding' and our 'senses' – not just the 'five senses', but the 'others' for which those are 'merely a foundation', and which are awoken by, and the means by which we perceive, 'all that is highest[,] best and beautiful' in people, in the material world and in the spiritual realm.[235]

Unfortunately, Taylor Mill did not give any detail as to how what she and Mill referred to elsewhere as the Religion of Humanity would manage this.[236] In *Utilitarianism*, Mill said that utilitarianism will fail to motivate people 'until, by

---

[233] *Ibid.*, 226.　　[234] *Ibid.*, 161.　　[235] *Ibid.*, 23.　　[236] Mill, Letter 126, 152.

the improvement of education, the feeling of unity with our fellow creatures shall be ... as deeply rooted in our character, and to our own consciousness as completely a part of our nature, as the horror of crime is in an ordinarily well-brought up young person'.[237] But he gives no details about what such an education might look like. Taylor Mill suggested that it would involve only showing good examples to children, and preventing them from being motivated by a spirit of 'emulation' or 'competition', which she saw as being 'fruitful sources of selfishness and misery' because they make 'every person[']s ideas of goodness and happiness a thing of comparison with some received mode of being good and happy'.[238] But this is not much to go on. Similarly, although discussing the positive possibilities for a Religion of Humanity, Mill did not give any details about the institutions it would involve.

Whether Taylor Mill would have described herself as a Deist, a Theist, a sceptic, an agnostic, an atheist or an adherent of the Religion of Humanity, she was disappointed with many contemporary 'anti-religious' arguments, and seems to have taken particular umbrage at those given by defenders of George Jacob Holyoake in the 'Journal of Freethought and Positive Philosophy', *The Reasoner*. (Holyoake was imprisoned for atheism in 1842.) 'I should dread for the furtherance of my anti-religious opinions the imputation that they do not admit of being better defended', she wrote.[239] She asked to see Mill's response to them 'if quite convenient' before he sent it off to the editors of *The Reasoner*. It was never published, so the manuscript may or may not accurately reflect Taylor Mill's thoughts as well as Mill's.

In the piece, entitled 'Enlightened Infidelity', Mill criticised anti-religious arguments which attached to idea of a 'Creator' of the world, because this was 'a matter for hypothesis and conjecture on which, in the absence of proof, people's judgement will vary according to the particular bias of their imagination'.[240] Instead, he felt the real mischief of religious views 'consists in identifying this Creator, with the ideal of abstract perfection, and making him, as such, an object of adoration and imitation'. Mill insisted that, looking at nature, we must admit that 'it has been made, if made at all, by an extremely imperfect being', and that it cannot support the idea of a 'just ruler ... unless that ruler is of extremely limited power, hemmed in by obstacles which he is unable to overcome'. 'Mankind', he added, 'can scarcely choose themselves a worse model of conduct than the author of nature', for '[n]one but a very bad

---

[237] Mill, *Utilitarianism*, 227.   [238] Taylor Mill, *Complete Works*, 142.   [239] *Ibid.*, 340.

[240] *Ibid.*, 159. Jacobs includes this piece in Taylor Mill's *Complete Works*, but we should be somewhat wary as the letter was written by Mill, and it is not clear whether this is a draft approved of by Taylor Mill or Mill's own draft which he gave her to look at, as requested in her letter, but which does not include her own opinions.

man ever manifested in his conduct such disregard not only of sufferings of sentient creatures, but of the commonest principles of justice in the treatment of them'. He was outraged that Christian writers asked us to worship a being which, on the one hand, created 'thousands of millions of sentient creatures foreknowing that they will be sinners', and, on the other, created 'a hell to torture them eternally for being so'.[241]

'Enlightened Infidelity' foreshadows Mill's final conclusion, in an essay published after his death, which was that it was not rational to believe in an omnipotent *and* omni-benevolent God, and the best position was one of 'scepticism' rather than either belief or avowed atheism.[242] Reason suggests, he said, that we can have 'Hope' in the existence of a benevolent, though not omnipotent, God, but not belief.[243] This may also have been Taylor Mill's position.

Two pieces of evidence suggest this was her position (both quite slim). The first comes from one of her letters written during her husband's final illness. About Taylor finally being free from pain for time she said, 'Thank God', adding in parentheses 'the good one who must abhor this wicked work of the demons as much as I do'.[244] (Earlier she referred to his suffering as being 'more such as one hears of the tortures inflicted by demons than anything else' – the 'demons' she refers to may therefore have been meant metaphorically, even if God was not.)

The second comes from an unpublished manuscript. Quoting a play by Joseph Addison,[245] she noted that 'the longing after immortality', which he ascribes to 'the divinity . . . stir[ing] within us', is the reason for 'the hope which is in us'. This 'hope' is the one referred to by St Anselm,[246] who said his reason for writing *Cur Deus Homo?* (or *Why God Became Man*) is the 'hope' for God's grace, love and existence. That is, Taylor Mill saw our apparently innate desire for 'perfection' as a spark of 'divinity' within us, and as a foundation for 'hope'

---

[241] *Ibid.*, 160. In response to the apologists' argument that 'good' did not mean, in reference to God, what it meant in reference to humans (and thus God could be 'omnibenevolent' even if, by human standards, 'a very bad man'), Mill famously said, 'I will call no being good who is not what I mean when I apply that epithet to my fellow creatures; and if such a creature can sentence me to hell for not so calling him, to hell I will go'. Mill, *An Examination of Sir William Hamilton's Philosophy*, 103.

[242] Mill, *Theism*, 429–89.   [243] *Ibid.*, 483.   [244] Taylor Mill, *Complete Works*, 366.

[245] Joseph Addison, *Cato, A Tragedy*, Act V, Scene 1. This was first performed in 1713 (and included a performance by an actor called John Mills), and was a success throughout England, being adopted by radicals as a play about opposition to tyranny. It is said to have had significant influence over key players in the American Revolution (containing versions of famous sayings from that period, including 'Give me liberty, or give me death!' and 'I only regret that I have but one life to lose for my country'). It is quoted by Edmund Burke in *Reflections on the Revolution in France*, and also by the fictional Wilkins Micawber in Charles Dickens' *David Copperfield* (1850). It is not unreasonable, therefore, to think this is the source for Taylor Mill's quotation, even if the play is not well-known today.

[246] At least, this quote and the first are *probably* from the sources I ascribe them, as Taylor Mill did not footnote her quotes, at least in unpublished works.

in the divine. She may, then, have had 'hope' in a good but not all-powerful God, though not 'belief'. Certainly, she did not agree with Catholic or most Protestant theology (or that of other religions).

As well as being critical of contemporary religion, Taylor Mill was highly critical of contemporary morality and social mores. She said that 'the word Virtue' had stood for 'many different & opposite practices and thoughts', but 'it has always answered the purposes of interested men to make it stand for this or that practice',[247] and (as noted in an earlier section) she was particularly critical of how what women were taught was 'virtue' supported and maintained the patriarchy. She was relentlessly critical of the way in which contemporary society crushed people's individuality, or 'crucified' them for having different opinions and trying to live a different life.[248] She felt that everyone had something to contribute to '[t]he science' or 'rather ... [the] art' 'of morals': 'for everyone may at least show truly their own page in the volume of human history, and be willing to allow that no two pages of it are alike'.[249] Both were of crucial importance – the one being the result of freely developing our individuality, and the other an acknowledgement of the need for toleration (as a positive, not a negative virtue), and a willingness to endorse the liberty principle.

This said, she wrestled with the extent to which we were permitted to 'resist ... laws, or customs which have the force of laws, with which we disagree'.[250] (We can see how this had personal importance for her own life, given her disagreement with the laws and customs regarding marriage, and her desire to resist them, without harming those she loved.) She had no real answer to the question of what might happen if *everyone* felt that they could disobey laws and customs with which they did not agree (especially as, she thought, everyone, at some point, must disagree with at least one law or custom). But she nonetheless asserted that 'if we are willing to endure the penalty we are justified in doing anything which we ourselves think right', and also that we could 'protest' the penalty inflicted on us (even if recognising that, in the eyes of those imposing it, that was the right thing to do). In much of her writing (most obviously *On Liberty*) she urged people to be active, to freely develop their individuality, to live their own lives by their own lights, and for society to allow them this freedom so long as they did not harm others (or make them unjustifiably unhappy), even if this meant breaking contemporary social codes.

She also urged caution when it came to blaming people for their actions.[251] Blaming people, was, she argued, 'the utmost assumption & ought to be regarded as involving one of the utmost responsibilities that a human being

---

[247] Taylor Mill, *Complete Works*, 148.   [248] *Ibid.*, 154.   [249] *Ibid.*, 141.   [250] *Ibid.*, 150–1.
[251] *Ibid.*, 155.

can undertake'. She was anxious that we look for the 'good' even in faults, and that we thought 'much and long and silently' and were sure we had 'all the links in the chain of evidence complete' before we 'arrive[d] at the conclusion that another is morally blameworthy'. She noted that plenty of people take pleasure in blaming others, and 'passing judgement' on them, but insisted this was often for 'wrongs' which 'are found to proceed more from absence of good than from presence of bad qualities' or 'in the majority of cases from a good feeling carried to the excess', which ought not to be blamed (or blamed in the same way) as actual moral wrongs. Moreover, she felt this pleasure taken in blaming was not good, and in a better society we would not do it.

Taylor Mill also dismissed a contemporary sentimentality that 'those are richest who have fewest wants', saying '[t]hose are richest who have most capacity for enjoyments and most means of obtaining enjoyment', and that the most virtuous were those who enjoyed most.[252] This 'most', though (as noted in an earlier section), was not just 'most' in quantity, though she evidently thought people should enjoy a variety of pursuits. Instead, she is speaking of 'most' in terms of quality, introducing to utilitarianism (and perhaps to Mill's *Utilitarianism*) the controversial concept of 'higher pleasures'.

She wrote, 'the higher the <u>kind</u> of enjoyment, the <u>greater</u> the <u>degree</u>'.[253] She suggested that 'perhaps there is but one class to whom this <u>can</u> be taught' as a maxim, at least at present, 'the poetic nature struggling with superstition' – superstition which might, from the context (about sex), be religious 'superstition[s]' relating to ideas around chastity, promiscuity and extramarital (or pre-marital) sex, but could refer to a range of social mores.

In *Utilitarianism*, Mill said: 'some *kinds* of pleasure are more desirable and more valuable than others. It would be absurd that … the estimation of pleasure should … depend on quantity alone'.[254] The Epicureans, Mill noted (very early utilitarians, on his account), 'assign[ed] to the pleasures of the intellect, of the feelings and imagination, and of the moral sentiments, a much higher value as pleasure than to those of mere sensation'. He himself argued that we could tell if something was a higher quality pleasure than some other pleasure by consulting the opinion of 'those who are competently acquainted with both', and who consistently 'placed [one] so far above the other that they prefer it', even if it is accompanied by a greater amount of discontent, 'and would not resign it for any quantity of the other pleasure which their nature is capable of'. He further argues that 'it is an unquestionable fact that those who are equally acquainted with, and equally capable of appreciating and enjoying, both, do give a most marked preference to the manner of existing which employs their higher faculties'. 'Few human creatures', he adds,

---

[252] *Ibid.*, 23–4, 226.   [253] *Ibid.*, 24.   [254] Mill, *Utilitarianism*, 211.

'would consent to be changed into any of the lower animals, for a promise of the fullest allowance of a beast's pleasures', and 'no intelligent human being would consent to be a fool, no instructed person would be an ignoramus, no person of feeling and conscience would be selfish and base', even if people told them 'the fool, the dunce, or the rascal is better satisfied with his lot than they are with theirs'. (Or, if they do 'fancy' they would exchange, this is 'only in cases of unhappiness so extreme, that to escape from it they would exchange their lot for almost any other'.)

These passages have led to a great deal of debate and controversy in utilitarian scholarship, which there is neither space nor time to enter into now. It is of interest, though, that this idea is found in a very early piece by Taylor Mill, and shows her potential influence in the development of Mill's utilitarianism. The idea of 'higher' pleasures is often dismissed as snobbery, but it need not be read that way in Taylor Mill's version (or necessarily in Mill's) – they are arguing that pleasures which engage our emotions, our imagination, our intellect and/or our concept of 'virtue' are more pleasurable than those which do not. This does not necessarily mean (as it is often taken) that Mill is saying opera is, for instance, better than rap, or football, or eating really greasy hamburgers. Mill did think that poetry was more pleasurable than the bar-game 'pushpin' – because poetry engages more of our 'higher' faculties than pushpin. He also believed that those who could appreciate poetry would not consent to a world in which the only entertainment on offer was bar-games. This has links back to Taylor Mill's arguments against 'sensuality', of course. To return to her initial example, we may or may not agree that sex which is solely directed at one's own pleasure is worse than sex where we are also very much concerned with the other person's pleasure, but it is not necessarily 'snobbery', which makes us decide one way or the other.

Overall, Taylor Mill was very concerned about questions of personal and social morality, and with the question of religion, both in the sense of the justification for personal belief and its social utility. Her writings on this topic are brief and generally underdeveloped, but they are still of interest, particularly in the history of the development of utilitarianism and the history of atheism. The idea of 'higher' pleasures is also one which can, and does, prompt contemporary thought and debate, along with the foundational question of whether utilitarianism is a moral system of ethical thought. Her addition of the caveat 'consistent with the happiness of all' to the idea of the 'greatest happiness of the greatest number' might also be fruitful ground for development by contemporary utilitarians.

8 Conclusion

Harriet Taylor Mill wrote on a wide variety of subjects, including political philosophy, ethics, religion and political economy. Her contributions have been greatly overshadowed by the fact of her close friendship with, and eventual marriage to, John Stuart Mill. Although it is true that his *oeuvre* is much larger than hers, however, we should bear in mind two things. Firstly, that Mill himself noted that much of his apparently 'single-authored' work was a joint production, with Taylor Mill taking a variety of roles (from editor to full co-author), with many of his ideas coming from a 'common' 'fund of thought' built up over many years of deep, intimate conversation about serious topics.[255] Secondly, that even without her contribution to some of Mill's work, Taylor Mill's output is not negligible, running to almost 600 pages (including letters). Even without her relationship with Mill, then, Taylor Mill ought to figure as a more prominent figure in the canon of the history of political thought, and her single-authored pieces reveal unique and nuanced arguments which repay study.

Mill recorded that she was his full co-author (or, perhaps more accurately, that he was hers) for *On Liberty*, one of the most famous books in the history of political thought. Although this was published a few months after her death, she played a significant role in its development and content, and we can trace several elements of its key ideas back to some of her earliest writings (along with some of Mill's earliest works) – the commitment to liberty, to independence and to the importance of 'the free development of individuality' to both their personal and political philosophies is clear from a very early stage, and remained a central theme of much of Taylor Mill's work, including her feminism and her economic theory.

She also played an important role in the development and structure of *Principles of Political Economy*. Mill notes that Taylor Mill suggested the need for the important chapter 'On the Probable Futurity of the Labouring Classes'; that the initial dichotomy which structures the chapter (the question of whether the poor should be dependent or independent) was hers and that much of the relevant passages were written in 'words taken from her own lips'; and that she helped set the whole 'tone' of the book.[256] This includes an account of her socialist thought, and her faith in the transformative power of workers-cooperatives.

In-between working with Mill on these two books, and co-authoring with him a series of articles on cruelty, tyranny, domestic violence and poor judicial decisions, Taylor Mill wrote and published *Enfranchisement of Women*, a series of powerful arguments for women's equality. She had a foundational belief that women and men ought to be equal in terms of rights and opportunities to maximise their individual happiness (consistent with the happiness of all) in particular through the free development of their individuality. This had

---

[255] Mill, *Autobiography*, 265.   [256] *Ibid.*, 255–7.

significant implications for their rights in relation to education, citizenship, employment, property, the person and the family. She identified how women were subjected by the patriarchy, and the way in which their gender was socially constructed in such a way as to render them inferior.

On a more personal level, Taylor Mill was a utilitarian who seriously considered her own faith and the rational basis of any belief in God. She also thought deeply about the nature of happiness, and individual obligations to sacrifice happiness if it meant breaking the law and rigid social conventions. This had particular personal bite given her relationship with Mill, and her marriage to Taylor, as well as her duties to her children.

As noted in Section 1, her two sons went to school once they were old enough, but her daughter, Helen Taylor, was – like most other women of her class – educated at home. After Taylor Mill's death, Taylor became Mill's companion, secretary and amanuensis. She inherited the copyright of both his and her mother's texts, and negotiated the publication of posthumous texts including the *Autobiography*, *Chapters on Socialism* and *Three Essays on Religion*, and re-publication of famous essays such as *Enfranchisement* and *On Liberty*.

Taylor was also very involved in practical campaigning for women's rights. She helped smuggle the petition for women's votes into Westminster so that Mill could present it in Parliament in 1866. She wrote her own defence of women's right to the suffrage (*The Claim of Englishwomen to the Suffrage Constitutionally Considered*) in 1867 (published, as *Enfranchisement* had been, in *The Westminster Review*). She also stood for election as an MP, getting sufficient names to secure a nomination, though this was refused by the returning officer as she was deemed ineligible because she was a woman.

Taylor found electoral success as a candidate for Southwark to the London School Board, being elected in successive elections in 1876, 1879 and 1882. Her programme included abolition of school fees; provision of food, shoes and stockings to needy children; abolition of corporal punishment; smaller class sizes; and more spending on the development of the child and the health of the teacher.[257] After she accused the manager of an industrial school of embezzlement and being responsible for the deaths of some pupils, she was sued for libel, in the end paying the plaintiff £1000, though the judge cleared her of personal malice and commended her public spirit. Her action (along with Elizabeth Surr and Florence Fenwick Miller) brought about reform of industrial schools in London.[258] Furthermore, she was active in the Irish Ladies' Land League, often

---

[257] See Smith, 'The Feminism and Political Radicalism of Helen Taylor in Victorian Britain and Ireland'.

[258] For more on this, and on Helen Taylor, see Levine, 'Taylor, Helen'.

chairing its meetings in both England and Ireland. She was also a leading member of the Land Reform Union and the League for Taxing Land Values.

In this, Taylor followed the radicalism of Taylor Mill and Mill, though of course in her own way and far more actively and publicly than her mother. (This was somewhat easier for Taylor to do, as an unmarried woman of independent means, than it had been for Taylor Mill given her non-traditional relationship with her husband, and with Mill. Taylor may also have been a more confident public speaker and performer than her mother, having trained as an actress in her youth, performing for several years under a stage name before her mother's death.) Taylor Mill and Mill, too, were very involved in the campaign for women's suffrage; supported land reform, and better policies (particularly towards landownership and individual rights) in Ireland; and wanted to reform education and end corporal punishment. We can see Taylor, then, as living out their legacy while also developing her own ideas and arguments. This included their commitment to socialism, as she was a founding member of the Democratic Federation, which was the forerunner of the Social Democratic Foundation (Britain's first organised socialist political party, with other early members including William Morris, George Lansbury and Eleanor Marx).

As well as this immediate impact on her daughter, Taylor Mill's *Enfranchisement* was also influential among early campaigners for women's right to vote, and was republished several times. Nowadays, of course, there have been two further 'waves' of feminism, and her arguments and insights can seem obvious, and her solutions a great deal less radical than they appeared at the time. Her feminist theory, therefore, is an often overlooked and interesting element of the history of the development of feminism, but probably has little impact on modern feminist thought. This said, her identification of the impact of the patriarchy on both women and men (and on violence in the home) still has salience, as do her critiques of traditional gender roles, and her explanation of why it is important that women can, and do, work.

Similarly, economics has moved on a great deal since 1848. This said, much debate in contemporary politics about economic questions does relate to the question of the extent to which economic institutions are made by humans (or 'natural'), and the related question of how much they can feasibly be changed, and/or are subject to questions of justice. That the laws of distribution are not as set in stone as the laws of production, and thus that socio-economic institutions can be changed and are an apt area for questions about justice, was one of the central insights which Mill credited to Taylor Mill in setting the 'tone' and outlook of *Principles*. Although the distinction was (rather unfairly) criticised by Marx,[259] it is a useful one for considering economic 'facts' as presented by politicians and vested interests, and also ideas for radical transformation.

Moreover, the central question of 'On the Probable Futurity of the Labouring Classes' – whether workers should be dependent on enlightened employers and charitable foundations or 'independent' – is still a live question. Debates continue about people's freedom and rights at work, and whether (and how) our working lives might become freer, more autonomous and more democratic. Similarly, discussions continue about what workers' 'fair' share in both management and profits is, and the different contributions (and how they ought to be remunerated) of 'workers', 'entrepreneurs' and 'owners' to profitability, the economy and society more broadly. Cooperation has not taken over the world in quite the way envisaged in *Principles*, but there are over three million cooperatives in the world; 12 per cent of the world's population are part of one; and they employ 10 per cent of the world's workers.[260] The International Cooperative Alliance alone represents over one billion cooperative members.

Taylor Mill may have thought that state ownership of the means of production, or organisation of labour, and state provision of benefits was a way of workers becoming more 'independent', in countries where states are democratic, and workers are all enfranchised. Or, she may have felt this was a different kind of 'dependency', even where workers had a say in who governed them, and how. This is hard to tell, because social democracy was not a form of socialism which she had experience of. The evidence from the later chapters of *Principles* (which discuss justifiable government action and interference in the market) is ambiguous – much state activity is seen as permissible, particularly running and owning industry which tends to monopoly, and providing welfare benefits. But such benefits might still be a sign of 'dependency', which it would be better to replace with working in cooperatives.

This said, her emphasis on 'the free development of individuality' *and* the need for greater social justice and, indeed, socialism is also an area of her thought with contemporary relevance. Her greatest legacy is probably through her contributions to *On Liberty*, which is frequently cited as a touchstone and foundational text of liberalism, and referred to in on-going debates over freedom of speech, thought and action. It is worth recalling, though, that when she and Mill wrote *On Liberty*, they saw themselves as socialists – socialists who emphasised individual independence, freedom and flourishing, but who *also* were committed to communal ownership of the means of production and a just

---

[259] For more on which, see Cohen, *Karl Marx's Theory of History*, 108–11 and Joseph Persky, *The Political Economy of Progress*, 157–60.

[260] See *International Cooperative Alliance* – www.ica.coop/en/cooperatives/facts-and-figures.

distribution of the product of collective labour. We can forget that there is this more 'liberal' strand in the history of socialism, identifying it only with authoritarian states. But it is a strand worth recalling and exploring.

Perhaps most importantly, Taylor Mill provides insight into a way of doing philosophy and political theory in a collaborative way. Often philosophers seem to be seen as individuals (generally men), who in glorious solitude (perhaps in ivory towers) come up with ideas entirely alone. The trope may be of Athena (goddess of reason) emerging fully formed from Zeus's head (with no input, of course, from a female deity or woman), or of Auguste Rodin's famous 'The Thinker'. Taylor Mill, by contrast, wrote philosophy (particularly in her younger years) around the demands of looking after a family and running a household (though we should not forget that she had at least some help from servants, given her class). Despite women not often being taken seriously at the time as interlocutors, she entered into in-depth discussions with Mill on a wide variety of topics, from ethics through to political economy, and they jointly built a 'fund of thought' on which both drew in writing a series of books which have become some of the most famous in the history of philosophy and of political thought. They wrote in a collaborative manner, sending each other manuscripts and working jointly on texts (and on editing already-published texts), to the extent of going through work sentence by sentence together and checking that it represented their real opinions.

In this process, and in their relationship, she and Mill seem to have seen each other a 'perfect equals', and tried to live out their principle of 'perfect equality' between the sexes. And this, too, is still a radical challenge to contemporary society in which women are not equal, and are particularly often not seen (or able to be) equals in intimate relationships or intellectual partnerships.

Indeed, it is still quite radical to recognise a woman's contribution to so seminal a work as *On Liberty* and to philosophy more generally (though women are generally recognised as having contributed to feminism, this is in itself often a devalued area of thought). In our own day, women make up only 19–26 per cent of philosophers at faculty level, and author only 12–16 per cent of publications in top-ranked journals.[261] Very few women are studied in the history of political thought, at least in introductory classes, which tend to focus on (white) men. Taylor Mill, though, belongs at the heart even of the usual introductory course, when we recognise her contribution to *On Liberty*, and seeing that text as collaborative and co-authored might change how students think about philosophy as a subject and an endeavour.

---

[261] Piovarchy, 'Philosophy's Undergraduate Gender Gaps and Early Interventions', 707–41.

Taylor Mill made a series of important contributions to feminist thought, utilitarianism, political economy and political theory. They are linked by her whole-hearted commitment to 'the free development of individuality', and belief that people ought to develop their own characters in such a way as to achieve the greatest happiness of the greatest number consistent with the greatest happiness of all. In this number they must not forget that they, too, counted (and of equal weight to all other individuals). Though this should not make them selfish, or act in ways which would cause unhappiness (or harm) to others, they ought to assert their rights to be active, self-developing individuals and citizens, and society ought to allow (indeed, champion and support) this attitude and work of development. They ought to strive to enjoy the 'highest' pleasures of which they were capable. In part, this necessitated 'negative' work of repealing unjust laws and social attitudes (for instance, those which currently made it illegal for women to study certain subjects or enter certain professions), and in part it involved more 'positive' work of building new institutions and passing new laws which would recognise women's human rights and allow everyone to live in a society in which they could be independent and equal, and where any inequalities present would be based on personal merit, not the 'accident' of sex or inherited wealth, and the associated privileges which allowed such accidents to give people significant advantages.

Taylor Mill's vision leaves us with many challenges today, as we cannot say it has so far been realised. We might not agree with all of her dreams or arguments, but we ought to be able to give reasons for not wanting to achieve her aims if we do disagree with them, as she provides a serious and significant challenge to much of the status quo which ought to provide much food for thought, and perhaps even inspiration for action, in the modern day.

Bibliography

Berlin, Isaiah, 'Two Concepts of Liberty' in *Four Essays on Liberty* (Oxford: Oxford University Press, 1969), 118–72.

Chambers, Clare, *Against Marriage: An Egalitarian Defence of the Marriage-Free State* (Oxford: Oxford University Press, 2017).

Cohen, G. A., *Karl Marx's Theory of History: A Defence* (Oxford: Clarendon Press, 1978).

Collini, Stefan, 'Introduction' in *Collected Works of John Stuart Mill*, XXI edited by John Robson (Toronto: University of Toronto Press, 1984), vii–lvi.

Crisp, Roger, *Routledge Philosophy Guidebook to Mill on Utilitarianism* (London: Routledge, 1998).

Deutscher, Penelope, 'When Feminism Is "High" and Ignorance Is "Low": Harriet Taylor Mill on the Progress of the Species', *Hypatia* 21/3 (2006), 136–50.

Hayek, Friedrich August, *John Stuart Mill and Harriet Taylor: Their Friendship and Subsequent Marriage* (London: Routledge, 1951).

Jacobs, Jo Ellen, '"The Lot of Gifted Ladies Is Hard": A Study of Harriet Taylor Mill Criticism', *Hypatia* 9/3 (1994), 132–62.

'Chronology' in *The Complete Works of Harriet Taylor Mill* edited by Jo Ellen Jacobs (Bloomington: Indiana University Press, 1998), xli–xliv.

Levine, Philippa, 'Taylor, Helen', *Oxford Dictionary of National Biography* (2004). https://doi.org/10.1093/ref:odnb/36431.

MacAskill, William, Darius Meissner and Richard Yetter Chappell, 'The Rights Objection' in *An Introduction to Utilitarianism* edited by R. Y. Chappell, D. Meissner and W. MacAskill (2022). www.utilitarianism.net/objections-to-utilitarianism/rights.

MacGilvray, Eric, *Liberal Freedom: Pluralism, Polarization, and Politics* (Cambridge: Cambridge University Press, 2022).

McCabe, Helen, '"Good Housekeeping?": Re-assessing John Stuart Mill's Position on the Gendered Division of Labour', *History of Political Thought* 38/1 (2018), 135–55.

'John Stuart Mill and Fourierism: "Association," "Friendly Rivalry" and Distributive Justice', *Global Intellectual History* 4/1 (2018), 35–61.

'Harriet Taylor' in *The Wollstonecraftian Mind* edited by Sandrine Bergès, Eileen Hunt Botting and Alan Coffee (London: Routledge, 2019), 248–60.

'Harriet Taylor' in *The Philosopher Queens* edited by Rebecca Buxton and Lisa Whiting (London: Unbound, 2020), 57–62.

'John Stuart Mill, Market Socialist?', *Review of Social Economy* 79/3 (2021), 506–27.

John Stuart Mill, Socialist (Montreal and Kingston: McGill-Queens University Press, 2021).

'"Political ... Civil and Domestic Slavery": Harriet Taylor Mill and Anna Doyle Wheeler on Marriage, Servitude, and Socialism', *British Journal for the History of Philosophy* 29/2 (2021), 226–43.

Mill, John Stuart, *Collected Works of John Stuart Mill* edited by J. M. Robson and others, 33 volumes (Toronto: University of Toronto Press, 1962–91).

Earlier Letters, XII and XIII (1963).

Principles of Political Economy, II and III (1965).

Auguste Comte and Positivism, X (1969).

Bentham, X (1969).

Theism, X (1969).

Utilitarianism, X (1969).

Whewell on Moral Philosophy, X (1969).

Later Letters, XIV and XVII (1972).

On Liberty, XVIII (1977).

Grote's Plato, XI (1978).

Two Publications on Plato, XI (1978).

An Examination of Sir William Hamilton's Philosophy, IX (1979).

Autobiography, I (1981).

Introduction to Enfranchisement of Women, 393–94 (1984).

On Marriage, XXI (1984).

Papers on Women's Rights, 378–92 (1984).

Statement on Marriage, XXI (1984).

Subjection of Women, XXI (1984).

Guizot's Lectures on European Civilisation, XX (1985).

Miller, Dale E., 'Harriet Taylor', *Stanford Encyclopaedia of Philosophy* (Spring 2018 ed.), Edward N. Zalta (ed.). https://plato.stanford.edu/archives/spr2018/entries/harriet-mill/.

Nozick, Robert, *Anarchy, State, and Utopia* (Oxford: Basic Books, 1974).

Persky, Joseph, *The Political Economy of Progress: John Stuart Mill and Modern Radicalism* (Oxford: Oxford University Press, 2016).

Phillips, Menaka, 'The "Beloved and Deplored" Memory of Harriet Taylor Mill: Rethinking Gender and Intellectual Labour in the Canon', *Hypatia* 33/4 (2018), 626–42.

Piovarchy, Adam, 'Philosophy's Undergraduate Gender Gaps and Early Interventions', *Ergo* 6/26 (2020), 707–41.

Robson, John, "Textual Introduction", *Collected Works of John Stuart Mill*, XXI edited by John Robson (Toronto: University of Toronto Press, 1984), lvii–lxxxiii.

Rossi, Alice, *Essays on Sex Equality: John Stuart Mill and Harriet Taylor Mill* (Chicago: University of Chicago Press, 1970).

Schmidt-Petri, Christoph, Michael Schefczyk and Lilly Osburg, 'Who Authored *On Liberty*? Stylometric Evidence on Harriet Taylor Mill's Contribution', *Utilitas* 34/2 (2022), 120–38.

Smith, Janet, 'The Feminism and Political Radicalism of Helen Taylor in Victorian Britain and Ireland', unpublished PhD thesis, London Metropolitan University (2014). https://repository.londonmet.ac.uk.

Stafford, William, 'How Can a Paradigmatic Liberal Call Himself a Socialist? The Case of John Stuart Mill', *Journal of Political Ideologies* 3/3 (1998), 325–45.

Stevenson, Ana, *The Woman as Slave in Nineteenth Century American Social Movements* (London: Palgrave Macmillan, 2019).

Taylor Mill, Harriet, 'Women (Rights of)', XXI (1984).

The Complete Works of Harriet Taylor Mill edited by Jo Ellen Jacobs (Bloomington: Indiana University Press, 1998).

Taylor Mill, Harriet and John Stuart Mill, 'The Acquittal of Captain Johnstone', XXIV (1986), 865–6.

'The Case of Anne Bird', XXV (1986), 1164–7.

'The Suicide of Sarah Brown', XXIV (1986), 916–19.

'The Case of Mary Ann Parsons' 1 and 2, XXV (1986), 1151–3, 1164–7.

Winch, Donald, *Wealth and Life: Essays on the Intellectual History of Political Economy in Britain, 1848–1914* (Cambridge: Cambridge University Press, 2009).

Cambridge Elements ≡

Women in the History of Philosophy

Jacqueline Broad
Monash University

Jacqueline Broad is Associate Professor of Philosophy at Monash University, Australia. Her area of expertise is early modern philosophy, with a special focus on seventeenth and eighteenth-century women philosophers. She is the author of *Women Philosophers of the Seventeenth Century* (Cambridge University Press, 2002), *A History of Women's Political Thought in Europe, 1400–1700* (with Karen Green; Cambridge University Press, 2009), and *The Philosophy of Mary Astell: An Early Modern Theory of Virtue* (Oxford University Press, 2015).

Advisory Board

Dirk Baltzly, *University of Tasmania*
Sandrine Bergès, *Bilkent University*
Marguerite Deslauriers, *McGill University*
Karen Green, *University of Melbourne*
Lisa Shapiro, *Simon Fraser University*
Emily Thomas, *Durham University*

About the Series

In this Cambridge Elements series, distinguished authors provide concise and structured introductions to a comprehensive range of prominent and lesser-known figures in the history of women's philosophical endeavour, from ancient times to the present day.

Cambridge Elements ≡

Women in the History of Philosophy

Elements in the Series

A full series listing is available at: www.cambridge.org/EWHP

Printed in the United States
by Baker & Taylor Publisher Services